LOW SALT ✦ DIET

AND

RECIPE BOOK

Beverly Barbour

A FIRESIDE BOOK
Published by Simon & Schuster, Inc.
NEW YORK

Manufactured in the United States of America

Pbk.   2 3 4 5 6 7 8 9 10

Library of Congress Cataloging in Publication Data

Barbour, Beverly, date.
Low salt diet and recipe book.
"A Fireside book."
Bibliography: p.
Includes index.
1. Salt-free diet—Recipes. 2. Salt-free diet.
3. Food—Sodium content—Tables. I. Title.
[RM237.8.B37   1985]   613.2'8   85-1539
ISBN 0-671-55745-9 Pbk.

To Renata,
who pitched in and never
let her blood pressure rise

CONTENTS

INTRODUCTION

We are besieged on every side by information, misinformation, scare headlines, and news bulletins implying that yet another of the foods we have long taken for granted is actually a slow form of poison—and we had better not eat it if we want to make it into the next decade. Sometimes they do not even allow us the luxury of a decade to succumb to the latest slow-death. It seems that cranberries may do us in this year and sugar the next. About the only thing remaining sacred is mother's milk—and Mom had better watch her eating, drinking, and smoking.

It is not only the media and the public who are confused. If you talk to enough doctors and medical researchers, you are almost always going to find two of them who will have diametrically opposed points of view on any given topic.

When the topic is salt, because salt seems to have a bearing on so many of the afflictions that assail our bodies, the one general consensus is that Americans, on the average, consume about four times more of it than they really need. Humans, and a lot of other animals, not only have a sweet tooth, they have a salt tooth as well!

And either one, or both, can keep you from growing "long in the tooth."

Does sodium deserve such a bad press? Not entirely.

The purpose of this book is to give you all sides of the story. There are doctors who feel that too little salt may be almost as dangerous as too much, and that for some lucky people there is never too much.

For those who know that they need to, or suspect that they should cut down on salt, this book has a wealth of information on how to go about doing so, including salt-free recipes and suggestions on adapting your own recipes by substituting other flavoring agents for salt.

You don't have to sacrifice eating pleasure to have a low-salt diet. Food is one of the few pleasures that last our lifetime. Let's live long and enjoy every morsel!

LOW SALT DIET AND RECIPE BOOK

CHAPTER 1

SALT AND HYPERTENSION

SALT IS ESSENTIAL

The fact that animals do not grow unless they have some sodium chloride was discovered by Harvard scientists at the beginning of this century. A certain amount of salt (sodium chloride, NaCl) is necessary to maintain life. Our bodies consist mostly of a saline solution. Salt water is man's natural environment, and when he evolved into a land being he interiorized his environment. As mammals, our cells are bathed in salt water.

Salt determines the volume of fluid retained in the extracellular spaces. It is the key factor in determining blood volume and therefore blood pressure. In postoperative patients, a solution of sodium chloride is almost routinely given intravenously to maintain fluid volume and protect against the need for blood. Moreover, replacing salt is an extremely important treatment for patients with a fever because they lose a great deal of salt in perspiration.

The presence of adequate amounts (or even surpluses) of sodium chloride in the diet provides protection against the consequences of specific stresses that can be life-threatening. These stresses include heatstroke and a variety of gastrointestinal infections and fevers in which there is fluid loss and diarrhea or vomiting.

These adequate amounts are easily supplied—too easily. Salt is a natural ingredient in almost every food Mother Nature provides for our tables, particularly vegetables and meats. Even before we reach for the saltshaker, our typical American diet contains four times more sodium than we need to maintain life. On top of that, about one quarter of the salt most people eat is added at the table.

MEDICAL RESEARCH ON SALT AND HYPERTENSION

Medical research has demonstrated that this excessive salt intake can sometimes affect high blood pressure. In the late 1950s Walter Kempner, professor of medicine at Duke University, and Lewis K. Dahl, senior scientist at Brookhaven National Laboratories and the Atomic Energy Commission, discovered that excessive salt intake can lead some susceptible bodies to the development of hypertension, also known as high blood pressure (the terms are interchangeable), which can lead to heart attacks and strokes. Because it is a factor in so many diseases that can be fatal, it is regarded as a major cause of death in the United States.

A renal specialist, Dr. F. M. Allen, published a textbook in 1920 on the treatment of kidney disease. The data showed the effectiveness of a low-sodium regimen in treating high blood pressure. But it was forgotten for the next twenty-four years.

In May of 1944, near the end of World War II, Walter Kempner presented the results of a new treatment he had devised for hypertension. His treatment was able to stop the damage hypertension brought to the heart, kidneys, and eyes in 140 patients. High blood pressure was reduced, enlarged hearts returned to normal size, damaged kidneys regained their function, and the progression of the disease—which can lead to complete blindness—was arrested. There were no harmful side effects. However, a major portion of the patients on the treatment did not continue it.

The treatment, a rice diet, was so boring and tasteless that patients found it difficult to stay on it. While treatment was going on, patients had to be hospitalized until blood pressure was controlled. When the patients or the hospital staff tried to modify the diet to make it taste better, blood pressure rose. More than a year of intensive study was required to discover why the rice diet worked, and then it was found that the rice was not the savior after all; it was the absence of salt that brought the amazing results. Here was Dr. Allen's twenty-four-year-old story retold.

Not all patients with high blood pressure can control their condition with a sodium-restricted diet, but in a twenty-five-year study at the Brookhaven National Laboratories researchers found that 25 to 33 percent of all hypertensive patients could be treated *by diet alone*. The remaining patients had better results with a treatment of diet and drugs, a combination that works better than drugs alone.

Diet is important, and a low-sodium diet today is considered basic in the treatment of high blood pressure.

In 1953 George R. Meneely of Vanderbilt University began feeding laboratory rats high-salt diets equivalent to the daily salt content of the average American diet. Many developed high blood pressure and died after seventeen months, although the rats' average lifespan is twenty-four to forty-eight months. Autopsies showed damaged kidneys and enlarged hearts, just as in humans with high blood pressure. The causes of death among the rats—strokes and heart attacks—were similar to those in hypertensive human beings. Furthermore, the time of life at which the rats became ill with the diseases paralleled middle age in humans.

But not all of the animals were affected, and subsequent breeding experiments carried on since 1954 by Lewis K. Dahl have indicated that high blood pressure is probably a genetic disease. Having developed a strain of rats that always developed hypertension, he then began feeding them salt-free diets and found that even with their genetic inheritance none of them gave evidence of the disease. When this was announced in 1962, it created a great stir in preventive medicine circles.

Can hypertension be controlled by limiting salt intake from childhood? Continuing studies done in many parts of the world certainly make it look that way. Lowering salt intake is a good move for anyone with a tendency toward hypertension—and maybe even for the population in general. But, like all diets, a low-sodium regime should be discussed with your physician; all types of high blood pressure are not alike and therefore cannot be dealt with as a single disorder.

Recent research has established that there are three distinctly different biochemical patterns among patients with hypertension depending upon whether the patient has lower than normal, normal, or high plasma renin levels. *Renin* is a protein-digesting enzyme released by the kidneys that acts to raise blood pressure. Low-renin patients respond particularly well to sodium depletion by diet or diuretic therapy (a diuretic tends to increase the output of urine). High-renin patients, on the other hand, may actually develop *increased* blood pressure with continued sodium depletion.

In our present state of knowledge, no one would recommend that all fever patients get the same medication, and doctors now know that this concept also applies to hypertension. Not all hypertension stems from the same cause and not all hypertension patients will benefit from sodium reduction. Some may be harmed.

The challenge for the physician is to analyze each individual patient and then apply the specific treatment that will be useful for that patient's type of high blood pressure. Hypertension can have many different causes, some of which involve excessive sodium in the body while others have no relation to sodium intake.

However, a majority of hypertensive people are labeled as suffering from "essential" hypertension. *Essential* means that the basic underlying cause for the high blood pressure has not been defined, and lowering salt intake is almost always prescribed.

CHAPTER 11

THE SALT HABIT AND WHAT IT'S DOING TO US

It is a habit shared by nearly all animals. Our four-footed friends look for a salt lick and lap it up. We head for the saltcellar or salty foods such as ham, potato chips, anchovies, or soy sauce and eat them up. The liking for salt may be, in part, inborn.

Just what is this attractive substance? "Salt" is the name given to forms of sodium chloride, NaCl. It occurs in the sea, in natural brines, and in its crystalline form it is known as "rock salt." All important salt deposits resulted from the evaporation of seawater at some point in history. Estimates are that if the entire ocean dried up it would yield fourteen and one half times more rock salt than the bulk of the entire European continent above the high water mark, including the Alps!

Because most forms of bacteria cannot survive in a high saline solution, salting or brining—the soaking of meats and vegetables in a strong salt solution so that the food is impregnated with salt—was one of the earliest methods of food preservation. Salt pork is an extreme example of heavy salting; the brining of pork before smoking it to produce bacon or ham is another. Probably the salting that began as a necessity developed the taste in our ancestors that accounts for our present-day peanut, popcorn, and potato chip craze.

It went so far, in fact, that we even put salt into baby foods, though babies really do not care. Mothers, who test the food for temperature or lick the spoons, buy what tastes good to them. So baby food manufacturers began salting to suit the mother's tongue. Hence, a taste for salt is acquired early by most youngsters. Later we wean them from baby food to salted crackers, and from there on it is an easy step to the heavily salted snack foods that make up a significant part of the American diet. (Fortunately, the consumer has become aware of the danger, and baby food processors have responded to pressure. There is no longer a problem in finding baby foods with labels clearly stating NO SALT ADDED. There is more of a problem finding labels that say SALT-FREE or LOW-SODIUM on other packaged or canned foods. But they, too, can now be found.)

As a result, salt addicts are now legion in most parts of the world. No other living mammal overdoses on salt as man does—and it is a habit resulting almost entirely from culture and customs acquired early in life and mostly at home. We seem to have lost the "instinct" for moderation that other mammals exercise. While our bodies do need some sodium to function well in this world, most of us get far too much of a good thing.

This need not necessarily be of great concern—unless a person has: a tendency to high blood pressure, someone in the family who has suffered from high blood pressure, certain heart problems (not necessarily associated with high blood pressure), or certain types of kidney disease.

CHAPTER III

HYPERTENSION AND STROKES

Here are some outstanding facts about hypertension, high blood pressure, and strokes. Later in this chapter we'll go into how salt can contribute to all these conditions.

- One out of every ten people interviewed in multiple national surveys conducted by the Bureau of Health Statistics of the National Institutes of Health was found to have high blood pressure (hypertension).
- Twenty percent of them did not know they had high blood pressure.
- Only 31.8 percent of the known hypertensives are under medical care. (Fourteen million of the 20 million who have it do not receive medical care.)
- Most Americans believe high blood pressure to be a benign, painless disease.
- Hypertension is the major cause of strokes.
- Strokes strike without warning.
- Hypertension is among the major causes of blindness.
- High blood pressure contributes heavily to the need for artificial kidneys and for renal transplants.
- The average person with hypertension remains in bed 8.8 days each year as a direct result of the disease.
- More than 9.5 million working days are lost annually because of high blood pressure. (This figure is inaccurately low since it does not include the disabled, the self-employed, and the unemployed.)
- High blood pressure is more common among black Americans than white.
- Hypertension can be induced in some animals by feeding them a large quantity of salt.

POSSIBLE AFTEREFFECTS OF A STROKE

- Paralysis of the right side of the body
- Paralysis of the left side of the body
- Paralysis of both sides of the body
- Blindness
- Inability to speak
- Inability to understand the spoken word
- Inability to chew
- Inability to swallow
- Inability to write

RULES TO LESSEN THE RISK OF STROKE

- Have blood pressure checked annually if you have no indication of hypertension.
- Have more frequent checks if you are pregnant, use oral contraceptives, and/or know you generally have a high blood pressure reading.
- Work down to a healthy body weight and stay there.
- Exercise regularly to condition the cardiovascular system and help control weight.
- Cut down on saturated fat and cholesterol consumption. (This will aid in weight control as well as help prevent arteriosclerosis.)
- Do not smoke cigarettes.
- Avoid people, places, and events that make you angry.
- Learn to deal with unavoidable stress through yoga, meditation, biofeedback, or psychotherapy.
- Keep sodium consumption under 2.5 grams per day (about ½ teaspoon).

WHAT CAUSES HIGH BLOOD PRESSURE?
True or False?

1. When parents or close relatives have high blood pressure, a person is more likely to develop the disease. *True.* When one parent has high blood pressure, there is a 50 percent chance that his or her offspring will have it. When both parents are hypertensive, the chances rise to 90 percent.

2. Hypertension is more common among white upper-class males in stressful jobs than any other segment of the population.

False. Hypertension is twice as common among the black population as the white. With blacks it comes earlier in life, is more severe, and causes more deaths at a younger age.

3. People who are overweight are more likely to develop high blood pressure.

True. Overweight makes the cardiovascular system work harder. Weight loss reduces blood pressure in all persons whether they are hypertensive or not.

4. Arteriosclerosis (the presence of fatty deposits on the inner walls of arteries) helps protect the walls of the blood vessels and prevents rupturing.

False. The fatty deposits, called "plaques," make the walls thick and irregular, in turn narrowing the blood vessels and increasing the pressure. This narrowing, particularly in the blood vessels of the kidneys, can promote high blood pressure.

5. A high blood sugar level can contribute to the complications of high blood pressure.

True. Diabetes mellitus, which is characterized by a high blood sugar level due to defective glucose metabolism, promotes arteriosclerosis.

6. Women who become hypertensive during pregnancy have a greater chance of developing hypertension later in life, even though their blood pressure may go down after giving birth.

True. Although blood pressure generally returns to normal, some women remain hypertensive. Even a temporary blood pressure rise during pregnancy may be the first sign of a tendency to develop high blood pressure later in life.

7. Salt can cause high blood pressure.

False—except in certain people who lose the ability to regulate or dispose of excess sodium; as a result the sodium remains in the body tissues, causing water retention and producing high blood pressure.

8. Habitual and excessive use of salt or products high in sodium raises blood pressure in some people who are susceptible to hypertension.

True. And it will aggravate hypertension in some who already have the disease.

9. Cigarette smoking raises blood pressure.

T

True. Chemicals in tobacco can cause arteries to constrict; this increases the pressure on the walls as the blood passes through.

10. Exercise raises blood pressure.

True. But only temporarily. A sedentary life-style contributes to obesity, which is one of the causes of high blood pressure. Regular physical activity can help lower the pressure.

F

11. Consistent stress becomes the norm and does not affect blood pressure, while occasional stress situations cause a temporary rise in blood pressure.

False. After occasional stress (such as an argument) the increased blood pressure will wind down. However, consistent stress, such as a stressful work situation, can become the norm and the job may cause a consistent rise in blood pressure.

F

12. High blood pressure can be cured.

False. Unfortunately, once you have it, the best you can hope for is to control your blood pressure enough to minimize the adverse effects of the disease, and if possible, eliminate the need for medication. *Exception:* There are a few people whose high blood pressure is the symptom of an underlying condition that can be cured.

It is not salt per se that gives doctors concern today; it is, of course, the sodium in the salt and other foods. Salt is sodium chloride (NaCl), our prime source of sodium. Table salt is approximately 40 percent sodium—there are from 2,200 to 2,300 milligrams (2.2 to 2.3 grams) of sodium in just one teaspoon of salt. An active adult in a temperate climate actually needs less than 2,000 milligrams of sodium per day. The level recommended as "safe" is 5,000 to 6,000 milligrams per day. Our average intake in America is 10,000 milligrams of sodium per day—more than four teaspoons of salt, more than four times our actual physical requirement.

Salt creates thirst and drinking liquid is nature's way of rinsing away the surplus sodium. This extra liquid loads the body with an additional volume of fluid for the kidneys to handle. Besides creating a thirst, sodium causes the tissues to hold fluid. This is beneficial and necessary, but when there is too much retention, the whole system has to work harder. After a salty meal the body of a healthy person and that of a person suffering from hypertension will both keep the amount of sodium required for maintenance. The balance will be excreted. It is not the salt itself, but what the sodium does to the body that causes high blood pressure. The kidneys play a major part in regulating blood pressure. Some doctors feel that a substance (the enzyme renin) secreted by the kidneys and passed into the bloodstream controls the build-up of pressure, and that sodium interferes with this secretion.

One of sodium's main functions in the body is that of working together with chlorine to regulate acidity and alkalinity (the pH) of your body fluids. When all is working as it should, the kidneys will excrete chlorine if the tendency is toward the acid side, and they will excrete sodium if the alkaline side is high. Sodium functions in regulating muscle contractions (charley horses) and nerve irritability; it also affects the permeability of cell membranes (the ease with which nutrients and waste pass through the cell wall).

When too much sodium is present in the body, the kidneys excrete it. If the body cannot get rid of the excess because of diseases of the heart, circulatory system, or kidneys, the sodium accumulates in the body and fluids accumulate with it. The result of this is *edema*, a swelling of the tissues because of fluid retention. Edema is an indication that the heart has to work harder, and this excess labor causes your blood pressure to go up. At this point a doctor usually recommends a restriction on the amount of sodium added to your body through foods, medicines, and liquids swallowed.

Excess sodium intake is not of concern to everyone. Many things determine who gets cardiovascular disease—a disease of the heart and blood vessels. Age, sex, color, heredity, exercise, weight—all may have an effect on the major diseases of the circulatory system: hypertension and *arteriosclerosis* (the narrowing of the arteries by deposits of fibrin and cholesterol along the arterial wall). According to a survey conducted by the National Center for Health Statistics from 1971 to 1975, approximately 17 percent of our adult population between the ages of twenty-five and seventy-four years have borderline hypertension (high blood pressure with a reading of up to 160 over 95), while 18 percent have definite hypertension (with a reading of more than 160 over 95).

Blood pressure is the force of the blood against blood vessel walls. Too much force can rupture blood vessels, cause kidney failure, blindness, strokes, or death. A blood pressure reading indicates two things: the pressure of the blood at the peak of the heart's contraction, when it is forcing the blood into the artery (called the "systolic" reading); and the pressure of the blood as it remains in the artery between contractions when the heart is resting (called the "diastolic" reading). The diastolic reading is the more important as it is less influenced by emotions, excitement, or exercise, and it should rarely read over 90. The systolic reading will change with age. A rough rule is to add your age to 100. If your reading is under the resulting number, you are fairly "normal."

In other words, if you are forty years old and your blood pressure is 140 over 90 (or less than these numbers), your physician will not be concerned about your blood pressure. Most doctors consider 120 over 80 as an adult average with 140 over 90 as a borderline between normal and high.

Hypertension is not a single disease entity; it can be the result of several abnormalities such as kidney disease, adrenal gland tumor, or blood vessel defect. Surgery or drugs can restore the blood pressure readings to normal for 5 to 10 percent of the people with this "secondary hypertension." In the remaining 90 to 95 percent of consistently high blood pressure readings, the cause of the disease called essential hypertension is unknown.

Hypertension is a major contributing factor in deaths resulting from heart attacks and strokes. Fewer than half of the people who suffer from high blood pressure are even aware that they have it, and probably many people who are aware that their blood pressure reading is a little high do not really understand what that means.

When the reading is consistently high and the doctor declares it is a good idea to restrict the sodium intake, you are in real trouble, because today sodium is found in almost all foods, almost all beverages (including drinking water) and in many medicines.

CHAPTER IV

IS IT POSSIBLE TO HAVE TOO LITTLE SALT?

Yes. Not everyone should restrict salt intake. The need for sodium in healthy bodies varies with age. The temperature, the humidity, and the degree of physical effort being expended (i.e., how hard you are working or playing) affect your need for sodium because they affect the amount you sweat. Salt leaves the body in urine and sweat. When our sweat glands go to work, they can pump us dry in a few hours, and if the sodium is not replaced, death can result. The estimated safe and adequate intake levels per day for sodium have been set at:

Infants (6 to 12 months old)	250–750 milligrams
Children (7 to 10 years old)	600–1,800 milligrams
Children (11 years and older)	1,100–3,300 milligrams
Very severely restricted low-sodium diet	200–400 milligrams
Severely restricted low-sodium diet	500–700 milligrams
Low-sodium diet	1,000–3,500 milligrams
Recommended adult diet	5,000–6,000 milligrams

As there are 1,000 milligrams in a gram and 1 level teaspoon of salt weighs approximately 4 grams (570 milligrams sodium per ¼ teaspoon), the total recommended intake is approximately:

Infants (6 to 12 months old)	⅛–¼ teaspoon
Children (7 to 10 years old)	¼–¾ teaspoon

Children (11 years and older)	½–2 teaspoons
Very severely restricted low-sodium diet	⅛ teaspoon
Severely restricted low-sodium diet	¼ teaspoon
Low-sodium diet	2 teaspoons–2 tablespoons
Recommended adult diet	8 teaspoons–3 tablespoons

If you suffer from: nausea, vomiting, dizziness, apathy, exhaustion, painful cramps, or poor circulation, the cause *may* be too little salt in the diet, or in some cases, low blood pressure. To cure the problem do *not* take salt tablets. Salt at mealtimes and in the water we drink will meet the needs of most people. However, if there is a prolonged shortage of salt, make a 0.1 percent salt and water solution (about ½ teaspoon salt dissolved in 1 cup water) rather than taking salt tablets. Excessive salt intake can be toxic, even fatal—but so can too little salt!

POTASSIUM

Unfortunately sodium is not the only nutrient we have to worry about; potassium is also of concern because sodium and potassium work together in the body's normal functioning. When we reduce our sodium intake we must be careful not to reduce the potassium. Generally, think of sodium as the bad guy in the black hat, and potassium as the good guy we want on our team. Fortunately, potassium is found in such everyday foods as bananas, figs, apricots, broccoli, cauliflower, corn, oatmeal (non-instant), and light table wine. If your doctor says, "Eat a banana every day," what he is probably saying is: "Increase your potassium." But here again we have a contradiction. Potassium chloride, a salt "substitute," when given as a supplement, has not been entirely satisfactory. Ulcerations of the gastrointestinal tract are well known adverse effects from some preparations of potassium chloride.

A much more important issue in considering potassium chloride as a substitute is its cardiotoxicity. Potassium has long been used to stop the heart for heart surgery, and large amounts of it taken orally can affect the plasma level very abruptly, and often unexpectedly. Too much potassium is actually more dangerous to everyone than too much sodium.

Dr. John Laragh, director of the Cardiovascular Center and Hypertension Center and chief of the Cardiology Division, Department of Medicine at the New York Hospital-Cornell Medical Center states: "The cardiotoxicity of potassium salt, while not so obvious or demonstrable in oral usage, poses such a serious potential hazard that, in my opinion, potassium chloride should never be used with impunity in the broad applications for which sodium chloride is now applied or at least until broad and careful testing controverts this weighty evidence."

IODINE

Many consumers are not aware that salt was chosen to carry iodine as a dietary supplement for iodine-deficient diets. There are geographical areas, known as "goiter belts," where the soil is deficient in iodine. The option of being able to purchase iodized salt has greatly decreased the incidence of goiter. In goiter belt areas anyone on a low-sodium diet may wish to consult his physician about adding iodine to the diet.

CHAPTER V

SALT LURKS IN UNLIKELY PLACES

Our bodies have varying degrees of tolerance for sodium. Some of us can eat as much as we wish with absolute impunity (or so it seems). Others will enjoy longer, more active lives if sodium is omitted entirely. Living sodium-free is a difficult task because salt does appear in foods which we don't think of as salty, and in medications, in public water supplies, in soft drinks, even in our toothpaste.

It does, indeed, lurk in unlikely places!

Check foods you think are high in sodium:

1. _____ Drinking water	11. ✓ Bread	
2. ✓ Baking soda	12. ✓ Dark rye flour	
3. _____ Apples	13. ✓ Dark brown sugar	
4. ✓ Beef	14. _____ Honey	
5. ✓ Ham	15. ✓ Catsup	
6. ✓ Soft drinks	16. _____ Tomato paste	
7. ✓ Lard	17. ✓ Spaghetti	
8. ✓ Margarine	18. _____ Rice ₽✓	
₽✓ 9. _____ Oatmeal	19. _____ Apricots	
10. ✓ Ready-to-eat breakfast cereals	20. ✓ Coffee	

Give yourself 5 points if you checked: 1, 2, 4, 5, 6, 7, 8, 10, 11, 12, 13, 15, 16.
Deduct 5 points for each error.
A score of 60 indicates a good eye or excellent tastebuds.

Once embarked upon a program to cut salt intake you must be constantly on your guard. Those little white crystals of salt and the component of salt you are concerned about—sodium—are lurking everywhere, even in medicines, "health" foods, and the local water supply.

Methods for measuring sodium in our daily diet are not completely standardized—all charts should be considered approximations. However, we do know what foods to avoid and which foods are low in natural sodium.

You will also note some strange contradictions. For example, shellfish (such as clams and oysters) are high in sodium, while the fish that have lived alongside them in the same ocean with nothing but salt water running over their gills are not high in sodium.

And heavy cream is much lower in sodium than skim milk.

Some vegetables are just naturally high in sodium, even when eaten raw or when boiled or steamed in unsalted water: celery, spinach, and beets are examples.

Recognizing which food is high and which is low in salt may seem complicated at first, but do not worry about it; once you have been on a low-sodium diet for a while and looked up the common foods a time or two, you will find you remember which are forbidden—and you will soon find others to replace them. You will be surprised at how many good things you can have—and there are many ways to flavor food without using salt (see Chapter VIII).

SALT IN MEDICATIONS

When it comes to medications, many drugs contain sodium. The following table was supplied by the High Blood Pressure Information Center and is taken from an article by Arthur G. Lipman, published in a 1980 issue of *Modern Medicine*.

Table 1. SODIUM CONTENT OF SELECTED NONPRESCRIPTION DRUGS (By Trade Name)

Product	Dosage forms	Sodium content*	Ingredients
Alka-Seltzer (gold box)	Effervescent tablet	552 mg/2 tablets	Sodium bicarbonate, citric acid, potassium bicarbonate
ALternaGEL	Suspension	2 mg/5 ml	Aluminum hydroxide
Aludrox	Tablet Suspension	3.2 mg/2 tablets 1.1 mg/5 ml	Aluminum and magnesium hydroxides
Amphojel	Tablet Suspension	2.8 mg/2 tablets 7 mg/5 ml	Aluminum hydroxide (300 mg each)
Basaljel	Suspension Capsule Tablet	2.4 mg/5 ml 5.6 mg/2 capsules 4.1 mg/2 tablets	Aluminum carbonate and hydroxide
Basaljel Extra Strength	Suspension	17 mg/5 ml	Aluminum hydroxide
BiSoDol	Tablet Powder	.072 mg/2 tablets 157 mg/teaspoonful	Calcium and sodium bicarbonates, magnesium carbonate, peppermint oil
Camalox	Tablet Suspension	3 mg/2 tablets 2.5 mg/5 ml	Calcium carbonate with aluminum and magnesium hydroxides
Chooz	Gum tablet	6.3 mg/2 tablets	Calcium carbonate, magnesium trisilicate
Creamalin	Tablet	82 mg/2 tablets	Aluminum and magnesium hydroxides
Delcid	Suspension	15 mg/5 ml	Aluminum and magnesium hydroxides
Di-gel	Tablet Liquid	21.2 mg/2 tablets 8.5 mg/5 ml	Aluminum hydroxide, magnesium carbonate, simethicone
Gelusil	Tablet Suspension	3.4 mg/2 tablets 0.8 mg/5 ml	Aluminum and magnesium hydroxides, simethicone
Gelusil-II	Tablet Suspension	5.4 mg/2 tablets 1.3 mg/5 ml	Aluminum and magnesium hydroxides, simethicone

*For comparison purposes 2-tablet and 5-ml doses have been used, but the reader should note that these are not necessarily equivalent doses. Refer to manufacturers' labeling for recommended doses.

Product	Dosage forms	Sodium content	Ingredients
Gelusil M	Tablet Suspension	5.6 mg/2 tablets 1.3 mg/5 ml	Aluminum and magnesium hydroxides, simethicone
Kolantyl	Tablet Gel	30 mg/2 tablets Less than 5 mg/5 ml	Aluminum and magnesium hydroxides
Maalox	Suspension	2.5 mg/5 ml	Aluminum and magnesium hydroxides
Maalox #1	Tablet	1.68 mg/2 tablets	Aluminum and magnesium hydroxides
Maalox #2	Tablet	3.6 mg/2 tablets	Aluminum and magnesium hydroxides
Maalox Plus	Tablet Suspension	2.8 mg/2 tablets 2.5 mg/5 ml	Aluminum and magnesium hydroxides, simethicone
Mylanta †	Tablet Suspension	0.043 mg/mEq of acid neutralizing capacity 0.054 mg/mEq of acid neutralizing capacity	Aluminum and magnesium hydroxides, simethicone
Mylanta-II †	Tablet Suspension	0.043 mg/mEq of acid neutralizing capacity 0.054 mg/mEq of acid neutralizing capacity	Aluminum and magnesium hydroxides, simethicone
Riopan	Tablet Suspension	1.3 mg/2 tablets 0.65 mg/5 ml	Magaldrate
Riopan Plus	Tablet Suspension	1.3 mg/2 tablets 0.65 mg/5 ml	Magaldrate, simethicone
Rolaids	Tablet	106 mg/2 tablets	Dihydroxyaluminum, sodium carbonate
Titralac	Tablet Suspension	0.6 mg/2 tablets 11 mg/5 ml	Calcium carbonate, glycine
Tums	Tablet	5.4 mg/2 tablets	Calcium carbonate, peppermint oil
WinGel	Tablet Suspension	5 mg/2 tablets 2.5 mg/5 ml	Aluminum and magnesium hydroxides

† Manufacturer does not express sodium content in milligrams per tablet or liquid dose. Instead, sodium content is expressed in mEq per acid neutralizing capacity.

Reference: Handbook of Nonprescription Drugs, Ed. 6, Washington, D.C., American Pharmaceutical Association, 1979.

Dr. Lipman is associate professor of clinical pharmacy and chairman of the department of pharmacy practice at the University of Utah in Salt Lake City.

Table 2. SODIUM CONTENT OF SELECTED NONPRESCRIPTION DRUGS*

Type of product	Trade names	Ingredients	Sodium content mg per dose	Sodium content mg per 100 ml
Analgesic	(Various)	Aspirin	49	—
Antacid analgesic	Bromo-Seltzer	Acetaminophen Sodium citrate	717	—
	Alka-Seltzer (blue box)	Aspirin Sodium citrate	521	—
Antacid laxative	Sal Hepatica	Sodium bicarbonate Sodium monohydrogen phosphate Sodium citrate	1,000	—
Antacids	Rolaids	Dihydroxy aluminum Sodium carbonate	53	—
	Soda Mint	Sodium bicarbonate	89	—
	Alka-Seltzer Antacid (gold box)	Sodium bicarbonate Potassium bicarbonate Citric acid	276	—
	Brioschi	Sodium bicarbonate Tartaric acid Sucrose	770	—
Laxatives	Metamucil Instant Mix	Psyllium Sodium bicarbonate Citric acid	250	—
	Fleet Enema	Sodium biphosphate Sodium phosphate	250-300 (absorbed)	—
Sleep-aids	Miles Nervine Effervescent	Sodium citrate	544	—
Antacid suspensions	Milk of Magnesia	Magnesium hydroxide	—	10
	Amphojel	Aluminum hydroxide	—	14
	Basaljel	Aluminum carbonate	—	36
	Maalox	Magnesium hydroxide Aluminum carbonate	—	50
	Riopan	Magnesium aluminum complex	—	14
	Mylanta I	Magnesium hydroxide	—	76
	Mylanta II	Aluminum hydroxide	—	160
	Digel	Simethicone	—	170
	Titralac	Calcium carbonate	—	220

*Reprinted by permission from table 4 of the American Medical Association's publication "Sodium and Potassium in Foods and Drugs" that was adapted from an article by D. R. Bennett, MD, PhD, entitled "Sodium Content of Prescription and Non-Prescription Drugs." Copyright (1979) to this information is held by the AMA.

SALT IN TOOTHPASTE AND MOUTHWASH

Toothpaste, tooth powder, and mouthwash all have sodium in their makeup. Rinse well, but do not swallow, and you will be all right. Or you can make your own sodium-free toothpaste by asking your druggist for chemically pure precipitated calcium carbonate. Combine that with a little glycerine each time you brush your teeth and your teeth will not be able to tell "homemade" from "store-bought."

SALT IN HEALTH FOODS

We think of textured soy protein, i.e., meat analogues, as being healthy; they, too, are often salt-ridden. *Consumer Reports* published the following partial listing in its issue of June

Table 3. SODIUM CONTENT OF SOME TEXTURED VEGETABLE PROTEIN FOODS

Brand name	Serving size (ounces)	Sodium per serving (milligrams)
Fearn Brazil Nut Burger Mix (dehydrated)	2.0	295
Worthington Frichik (canned)	3.2	665
Worthington Vegetarian Fillets (frozen)	3.5	50
Ganesh's Baba Burgers (frozen)	3.0	410
Fantastic Foods Nature's Burger Mix (dehydrated)	2.9	370
Loma Linda VegeBurger (canned)	3.8	390
Worthington Vegetable Skallops (canned)	3.0	580
Essence Natural Foods Harvest Steaks (frozen)	4.5	25
Earthwonder Millet Stew (dehydrated)	7.4	20
Cedar Lake Meatless Sloppy Joe (canned)	4.0	790

NOTE: Foods were rehydrated where applicable.

1980. For further information about specific brands contact the manufacturers.

SALT IN THE WATER SUPPLY

The salt in your water may come from natural salts found in the soil; from fertilizers in nearby fields that seep down into the water table, or run off into the river; from the salt used to de-ice winter streets that eventually finds its way into the soil; from your own water softener. You can buy devices that remove salts from water. These attach to your faucet and the water from them should be used for cooking as well as for drinking. Or, buy distilled water.

You can ascertain the sodium content of your local water supply by calling the Health Department; bear in mind that the reading may change with the seasons (from the salt on the streets, for example). Let the Health Department know that you want to be kept informed. When you are traveling, you can check the following table to give you some idea whether or not it is safe to "take the waters."

Table 4. PUBLIC WATER SUPPLIES (milligrams of sodium in 8 ounces [one cupful]

Aberdeen, South Dakota	48.0	Carson City, Nevada	0.9
Albany, New York	0.4	Charleston, South Carolina	2.3
Albuquerque, New Mexico	12.0	Charleston, West Virginia	0.7
Annapolis, Maryland	0.4	Charlotte, North Carolina	0.7
Ann Arbor, Michigan	4.8	Charlottesville, Virginia	0.4
Atlanta, Georgia	0.4	Cheyenne, Wyoming	0.7
Augusta, Maine	0.4	Chicago, Illinois	0.7
Austin, Texas	7.2	Cincinnati, Ohio	1.6
Baltimore, Maryland	0.7	Cleveland, Ohio	2.3
Baton Rouge, Louisiana	21.6	Columbia, South Carolina	0.9
Beloit, Wisconsin	1.1	Columbus, Ohio	12.0
Biloxi, Mississippi	55.2	Concord, New Hampshire	0.4
Birmingham, Alabama	4.8	Crandall, Texas	408.0
Bismarck, North Dakota	14.4	Dallas, Texas	7.2
Boise, Idaho	4.8	Denver, Colorado	7.2
Boston, Massachusetts	0.7	Des Moines, Iowa	2.3
Brownsville, Texas	14.4	Detroit, Michigan	0.7
Buffalo, New York	1.6	Dover, Illinois	4.8
Burlington, Vermont	0.4	Durham, North Carolina	0.9

El Paso, Texas	16.8	Newark, New Jersey	0.4
Evansville, Indiana	4.8	New Haven, Connecticut	0.7
Fargo, North Dakota	12.0	New Orleans, Louisiana	2.3
Frankfort, Kentucky	0.7	New York, New York	0.7
Galesburg, Illinois	72.0	Oakland, California	0.7
Galveston, Texas	81.6	Oklahoma City, Oklahoma	23.6
Harrisburg, Pennsylvania	0.4	Olympia, Washington	1.1
Hartford, Connecticut	0.4	Omaha, Nebraska	18.8
Helena, Montana	0.7	Philadelphia, Pennsylvania	4.8
Houston, Texas	38.4	Phoenix, Arizona	25.9
Huntington, West Virginia	7.2	Pierre, South Dakota	21.6
Indianapolis, Indiana	2.3	Pittsburgh, Pennsylvania	14.1
Iowa City, Iowa	1.1	Portland, Maine	0.4
Jackson, Mississippi	0.9	Portland, Oregon	0.2
Jacksonville, Florida	2.3	Providence, Rhode Island	0.4
Jefferson City, Missouri	7.2	Raleigh, North Carolina	0.9
Jersey City, New Jersey	0.7	Reno, Nevada	1.1
Kansas City, Kansas	9.4	Richmond, Virginia	1.6
Kansas City, Missouri	23.6	Rochester, Minnesota	1.6
Lansing, Michigan	2.3	Rochester, New York	0.7
Lincoln, Nebraska	7.2	Sacramento, California	0.7
Little Rock, Arkansas	0.2	Santa Fe, New Mexico	0.9
Los Angeles, California		St. Louis, Missouri	12.0
aqueduct source	14.1	St. Paul, Minnesota	1.1
metropolitan source	40.1	Salem, Oregon	0.4
river source	12.0	Salt Lake City, Utah	1.8
Louisville, Kentucky	4.8	San Diego, California	12.0
Madison, Wisconsin	0.9	San Francisco, California	2.3
Manchester, New Hampshire	0.4	Seattle, Washington	0.4
Marion, Ohio	40.8	Sioux Falls, South Dakota	2.3
Memphis, Tennessee	4.8	Springfield, Illinois	1.8
Miami, Florida	4.8	Syracuse, New York	0.4
Milwaukee, Wisconsin	0.7	Tallahassee, Florida	0.7
Minneapolis, Minnesota	1.1	Topeka, Kansas	2.3
Minot, North Dakota	60.0	Trenton, New Jersey	0.2
Montgomery, Alabama	1.8	Tucson, Arizona	7.2
Montpelier, Vermont	0.2	Washington, D.C.	0.7
Nashville, Tennessee	0.7	Wichita, Kansas	12.0
Nevada, Missouri	77.8	Wilmington, Delaware	1.8

CHAPTER VI

FORBIDDEN FOODS AND EAT-YOUR-FILL FOODS

FORBIDDEN FOODS

It is very difficult to measure the sodium content of various foods because it will vary from region to region depending on the soil, water (if used for irrigation), and fertilizers. But, generally speaking, here are the foods to be avoided. An asterisk (*) beside a food means you can have it only if the brand specifically says "salt-free" or "low-sodium," or if it is made without salt.

Beverages

Buttermilk*
Carbonated drinks (club soda, colas, Fresca, Dr Pepper, ginger ale, 7 Up, etc.)
Chocolate milk
Cocoa (instant)
Milk shakes

Baked Goods and Griddle Cakes

Bread*
Cakes and cake mixes*
Cookies and cookie mixes*
Crackers
Crepes*
Pancakes*
Rolls or muffins*
Salted snack foods
Waffles*

*Dairy Products**

Aerosol whipped toppings
Butter*
Cheese*
Ice cream*
Nondairy creamers
Sherbet*

Fish

Anchovies
Canned fish*
Caviar
Clams
Cod, dried or salted
Crabs
Frozen fish fillets
Herring
Lobster
Salted fish
Sardines
Scallops
Shellfish (except oysters, if physician allows)
Shrimp
Smoked fish

Flavorings

A.1. sauce
Bouillon cubes*
Catsup*
Celery flakes and celery salt
Chili sauce*
Chutney
Cocoa (instant)
Garlic salt
Gelatin, flavored
Horseradish*
Lemon pepper
Mayonnaise*
Meat extracts
Meat tenderizers*
Molasses
Monosodium glutamate and seasoning salts based on MSG
Mustard*
Olives
Onion salt
Pickles*
Relishes*
Rennet tablets
Salt
Salted nuts
Salt substitutes (except what your doctor allows)
Soy sauce
Sugar substitutes (cyclamate sodium)
Worcestershire sauce

Meats

Bacon
Bologna
Brains
Canned meat and meat-based soups and stews*
Chipped beef
Frankfurters
Ham (except canned low-sodium)
Kidneys
Kosher meats
Liverwurst
Pickled meat
Salami
Salted meat
Salt pork
Sausage
Smoked meat
Spiced meat

Staples

Baking powder
Baking soda (sodium bicarbonate)
Cereals, quick cooking and dry
Flour, rye and self-rising
Lard
Sugar, dark brown
Syrups, flavored

Vegetables

Artichokes
Beets (including greens)
Canned vegetables and
  vegetable soups*
Celery
Dandelion greens

Dried fruits (if sodium sulfide
  is on the label)
Kale
Lima beans, frozen
Mustard greens
Peas, frozen
Sauerkraut

EAT-YOUR-FILL FOODS

Now that you have looked at all the things you cannot have
you may feel the future's not worth facing—but that is not the
case. Actually, our sturdy pioneer forebears got along without
almost all of those salt-laden foods, and ate well, too. So can
you! Just see all the good things left on your "allowables" list.
When in doubt, check the specific sodium-content lists in the
Appendix. An asterisk (*) next to a food means it *must* be a
sodium-free or low-sodium brand, or made without salt.

Beverages

SOFT:
Apple cider
Apricot nectar
Buttermilk*
Cream, heavy and light
Fruit juices
Seltzer water

ALCOHOLIC:
Beer (not ale)
Cordials
Liqueurs
Spirits
Wines (red and white)

Baked Goods and Griddle Cakes

Bread*
Cookies*
Crepes*

Muffins*
Pancakes*
Waffles*

Dairy Products

Butter*
Cheese*
Ice cream*

Sherbet*
Yogurt*

Fish/Seafood

All freshwater varieties,
  cooked without salt

All saltwater varieties not on
  the Forbidden list, cooked
  without salt

Flavorings

Bouillon cubes*
Carob
Catsup*
Chili sauce*
Herbs, natural and
   unadulterated
Horseradish*
Lemon juice and other fruit
   juices
Mayonnaise*

Meat tenderizer*
Mustard*
Pickles*
Relishes*
Salt substitutes (if your doctor
   permits)
Spices, natural and
   unadulterated
Tomato paste*
Yogurt

Fruits

All are allowed

Meats

Beef (in small amounts)
Chicken
Duck
Lamb (in small amounts)

Mutton (in small amounts)
Pork (in small amounts)
Rabbit
Turkey

Vegetables

All that are not on the
   Forbidden list

So, you see, the picture is not all that gloomy after all! With a little imagination and creativity you can eat sumptuously on a salt-free diet. And later, in Chapter XI, you will find the recipes that will help you get started on the path to a cuisine that is low in salt and high in flavor.

CHAPTER VII

HOW TO "EAT OUT" SALT-FREE

When you leave the U.S.A. and want to eat as little sodium as possible, communication becomes a problem. When you do not leave home, but have to eat out, it is a problem, too, but at least you are conversant and can usually get the message across that "Dammit, I can't eat salt."

So type a list for your wallet of the polite expressions that will allow you to eat *sans* salt almost anywhere. When the natives take your pronunciation with a grain of salt, let them read the list—they usually get the idea.

Arabic	*bidoun malh*	Japanese	*shio nuki*
Chinese	*wu yen*	Lithuanian	*be druskos*
English	without salt	Portuguese	*falto de sel*
French	*sans sel*	Russian	*bez soli*
German	*ohne Salz*	Spanish	*sin sal*
Greek	*horis alati*	Swedish	*utan salt*
Italian	*senza sale*	Yiddish	*una zaltz*

RESTAURANTS

It is really not as hard as it sounds. Most restaurants and private clubs will be happy to help and will prepare special items for you if you ask them in advance. They do, after all, want you to come back.

It is usually best to skip the vegetables—which is not too hard to do inasmuch as most restaurants cook them, or hold them in a steam table, to the point where all flavor, texture, and vitamins have long since disappeared. Many chefs automatically add salt to the water vegetables are cooked in, and a few will also add a pinch of baking soda (sodium bicarbonate), because, although it does destroy vitamins, it also helps keep green vegetables green. Then, too, some restaurants just open a can and most of those vegetables are salted during the canning process.

Skip the bread, too, unless the restaurant has unsalted matzohs or you have brought your own low-sodium bread with you. And do not order soup, as it is always salted.

Baked potatoes or rice would be a fine substitute for the bread, but skip the butter unless it is "sweet" (unsalted), and avoid the bacon bits and the cheese. Use pepper and paprika for seasoning, or chopped onions and fresh parsley.

Do not order fish unless you know it is fresh (frozen is often dipped in brine before freezing), and then order it steamed or fried in oil and specify "unsalted." For flavor use lemon and/or dill or even vinegar (British fashion).

Any roast except ham (though beef is higher in sodium than veal, lamb, or pork) should be fine if you specify an inside cut—the chef may have salted the outside before roasting. Skip the gravy.

White meat is preferable to dark when it comes to chicken or turkey, and do not eat the skin. Query the waiter to be certain that it does not come on a bed of sauce, or covered with some sort of gravy. Cranberries are a delicious substitute for gravy.

Grilled steak, lamb chops, or pork chops ordered strictly unsalted are always available and so is a salt-free omelet. You could ask the chef to sprinkle the chop with ginger.

Salad is a bonanza. Oil and vinegar in cruets or fresh lemon are about the only kind of dressing you can order in most eateries. Cheese dressings are out and most of the other prepared dressings will have salt in them. No mayonnaise allowed either, of course.

Chinese food is fine for low-sodium eaters, provided you skip the soy sauce and tell the waiter very clearly and emphatically: no MSG (monosodium glutamate) and, of course, no salt.

Fresh fruit or baked apple is your best bet in the dessert department. Maybe fresh fruit pie, provided you lick the crust clean and leave it on your plate, or have sherbet or ice cream.

Do not be afraid to bring anything of your own to a restaurant (including a pill box of mixed herbs for seasoning salads, vegetables, and starches). I was in a posh New York restaurant recently when a woman at the next table pulled out a rather sizable container of her favorite brand of instant decaffeinated coffee. Not one of the tuxedo-clad staff blinked an eye.

FAST FOOD OPERATIONS

It is surprising, but they will often "hold the salt" for you. You probably will not be the first to ask.

AIRLINES

Request low-sodium meals when you make your airline reservations. Most airlines today have special diets available (fortunately they are usually better than the regular fare). You must ask the stewardess for your special tray when meals are served.

When the plane carries only salt-laden foods, dig into your purse and pull out low-sodium cheese, salt-free crackers, and fruit—you will survive. As soft drinks and club soda all have sodium, you will perhaps have a greater problem finding a salt-free beverage . . . there is always white wine.

Search out hotels with rooms that have refrigerators where you can store your own emergency food supply, including salt-free water. When rooms have no refrigerator, explain that you are on a strict diet and must carry certain foods with you. The management is always understanding. You may even be able to put your food in a kitchen refrigerator. (Bear in mind that the cleanup men and busboys raid the refrigerators at every opportunity, and there is always the chance that your food will vanish overnight.)

HOMES

Here you may have a problem. No one enjoys having you turn up with your own meal in hand (although superstar

Carol Channing does exactly this no matter where she goes—
including the White House!). You may feel conspicuously different from the others, and the hostess may feel she should
have prepared a salt-free meal even though you assured her
she should not have. If your sodium restriction is not too
strict, perhaps the thing to do is snack well before arrival, push
around small portions at the dinner table, and be extra careful
for the next three or four days, as it takes about that long for
your body to rinse away the sodium. When the hostess is a
close friend, tell her that roasts, steaks, or chops without salt
are best for you.

You could also offer to bring along the entree, dessert, or
some part of the meal that you can prepare salt-free. Since you
are using other flavorings to make the dish taste good, no one
will be the wiser and you will have at least one dish that you
can eat a lot of with a clear conscience.

PICNICS

Skip the hot dogs and the salami; instead, concentrate on
the hamburgers or cold breast of chicken, potato salad made
with your own dressing, raw vegetables, and your own dessert.
Bring your own bottle of wine, fruit juice, seltzer, or a combination of any two.

CHAPTER VIII

HOW TO COOK WITHOUT SALT AND ENJOY IT

The first step in cooking without salt is to realize that most of us are addicted to it and that it is going to take an adjustment period for our taste buds to be weaned. About one-fourth of those who suddenly drastically discard the saltshaker go through a minor withdrawal syndrome the first week. The symptoms are nervousness, tiredness, and mild depression. After ten days the symptoms have generally departed. An addiction to salt is similar to other addictions we create with caffeine, tobacco, drugs, or alcohol.

On the plus side, about a quarter of the people with backbone who pare down their salt intake seem to feel that the world has become a more pleasant place, and this feeling is translated into better relationships within the family and even in dealing with the public.

Cooking without sodium sounds easy—you just lock up the saltshakers or, if your doctor allows, fill them with potassium chloride which will pass in cooking, but is somewhat bitter. But eating without salt is not easy at all. Sodium lurks in the most unlikely places. And sometimes it is sneaked in: A label may say NO SALT or LOW SALT, and then you will find the word *sodium* slipped in between the pepper and the vinegar on the ingredient list. So keep your eyes open, read carefully, and do not miss a trick.

When you first go on a low- or no-sodium diet, do not start by preparing your favorite dishes *sans* salt and do not buy salt-free products such as chili and soup and cheese. They are just not going to taste the same. Instead spend the first two of your weeks "off the salt" making your own basics and getting involved in doing it yourself. It is somehow easier to maintain enthusiasm and interest if you are playing the salt-free cooking game than if you are just a critical taster of salt-free foods.

At first you will find that the foods having the most natural flavor are the most appealing. Cookbook author Craig Claiborne, after he had been on a salt-free regime for some time, declared that onions, tomatoes, eggplant, and mushrooms seemed to have the most taste. The beauty of all of them is that they mix and match with so many other foods and carry their flavor with them. Then, too, all of them take very kindly to herbs.

Dr. Mel Magida, who treats a lot of hypertensive patients in his Stamford, Connecticut, practice, eats very little salt himself and recommends to his patients that they do a lot of their cooking on a grill, as the flavor of charcoal or hickory is a wonderful substitute for salt. He also recommends "lots of raw onion, garlic, and lemon juice."

SUGGESTIONS FOR ADAPTING RECIPES
Aspics/Gelatin Salads and Desserts

Use unflavored gelatin and combine it with salt-free fruit juices, meat or fish stock you have made yourself (or from low-sodium bouillon cubes). For flavor accent use vinegar, lime or lemon juice.

Baking

Make your own baking powder (see Chapter IX, "Sodium-free Basics You Can Make or Buy). When baking soda is called for, be sure to use potassium bicarbonate and not sodium bicarbonate. It is the bicarbonate that actually carries the carbon dioxide needed to raise your cake, so you use exactly the *same* amount no matter which variety you are working with.

Beverages

Commercial soft drinks are salted and so are some bottled waters. The latter differ so widely that to be certain of what you are drinking it is wise to write the company and ask them for an assay of their product; they have these readily at hand and are very obliging in providing them upon request. Because natural springs differ so widely in mineral content, depending upon their location and the nature of the surrounding soils, this individualized approach is the only effective one for being sure. Since it is impossible to trace the water sources of soft drinks, it is best to make suitable substitutes by combining salt-free seltzer water with fruit juices. You can make a variety of palatable "spritzers" with natural juices, nectars (a term that generally denotes inclusion of the mashed pulp of juicy fruits), or apple cider. A dash of fresh lemon or lime juice does wonders for most fruit drinks, as do extracts such as peppermint, anise, almond, and spearmint. Cloves and cinnamon are good with cider, apple, peach, and pear juice.

Canning

When a recipe calls for a small amount of salt, it is added just for flavor, as in canning vegetables, so you can safely omit it. However, if it is a heavy brine formula (salt and water solution) as in making pickles or preserving meat, you may have to pass the recipe by as the large measure of salt is actually a preservative and to omit it could possibly cause food spoilage. Nothing is worth risking death by botulism.

INGREDIENTS THAT NEED WATCHING
Bacon

There is a product on the market called Bakon Yeast that does taste remarkably like bacon—particularly after the first couple of weeks when your taste buds have forgotten some of the salt flavor. You can use this in salads and casserole dishes or sprinkle it on sandwiches.

Chocolate

Most chocolates and cocoas are sodium carriers, but not Hershey brand cocoa. You can use it in any recipe calling for cocoa and in any recipe calling for chocolate. (See Chapter IX, "Sodium-free Basics You Can Make or Buy.")

Cream

Do not use nondairy creamers or anything coming out of an aerosol can. The heavier the cream the less sodium.

Flour

All flours can be used except self-rising flour, which has both salt and baking powder in its formula. Avoid it! And when possible, choose light rye flour, as a little sodium is present in the dark rye flour.

Fruit

Most is fine when fresh or if allowed to dry naturally. Canned or frozen may have salt added, so check the label or buy in the health food or diet section of the store.

Margarine

Fleischmann's has a salt-free green label and health food stores have "soy spreads." When you use margarine to sauté, add a few drops of vegetable oil and it will act like butter. The spreads should not be used in baking as air displaces some of the fat and your cake or cookie will not be as good.

Milk

It is best to use reconstituted low-sodium milk powder. You will not know the difference in baking, though you may (some do, some do not) if you love to drink milk. Check with your doctor; if your diet is not too strict, he may allow milk. Skim milk has more sodium than 2 percent, and 2 percent has more than whole milk. However, whole milk has more calories.

Salt

Lemon, lime, and orange juice and rind, herbs, spices, liqueurs, spirits, and vinegar are all substitutes. You will have to taste your way along as to quantities and which will best blend with the flavor of the dish being prepared.

Sauces and Gravies

You do not have to give them up, but make them with reconstituted low-sodium milk (watch carefully as it scorches more easily than milk does), your homemade stock, or low-sodium bouillon cubes. You can buy low-sodium cream soups that can be diluted and doctored up to make a decent sauce.

Sherbets and Ices

If salt is called for, substitute lemon, orange, or lime juice, or any of the liqueurs or spirits.

Sugar

All are okay except dark brown; substitute light for dark in the same amount.

CHAPTER IX

SODIUM-FREE BASICS YOU CAN MAKE OR BUY

More and more foods are available in sodium-free form, but not all foods and not always where you live. Health food stores are good sources for some, but in the event they are hard to find—or that you are a real adventurer—here are some you can make yourself or have prepared by a druggist.

THE SUBSTITUTES

Bacon

To add a baconlike flavor to salads, salad dressings, sauces, omelets, and breads, add Bakon Yeast (which is dried torula yeast). Add it also to unsalted butter or margarine to enhance steamed vegetables. The product is of vegetable origin and is acceptable on the most severely restricted salt- and sugar-free diets. There are less than 10 milligrams sodium per 100 grams. A rounded teaspoonful (about 100 grams) has only 12 calories.

Baking Powder

56.0 grams (approximately 2 ounces) cornstarch
15.0 grams (approximately ½ ounce) tartaric acid
79.5 grams (approximately 3 ounces) potassium bicarbonate
112.5 grams (approximately 4 ounces) potassium bitartrate

Combine above ingredients. When using this formula in recipes that call for regular baking powder, increase the amount you use by one-half. Example: If the recipe calls for 1 teaspoon of baking powder you would substitute 1½ teaspoons of this low-sodium mixture.

Baking Soda

Sodium bicarbonate is "regular" baking soda; substitute instead *potassium* bicarbonate, which you can buy from your drugstore. Use this in the same amount as you would sodium bicarbonate. Potassium bicarbonate gets hard when damp, so store it in a dry place in a tightly covered jar. If it does harden, scrape away until you have in powdered form the quantity your recipe calls for.

Bread

If you are lucky, a neighborhood baker may bake some salt-free bread for you and you can stock the freezer. Be certain he uses distilled water or reconstituted low-sodium milk powder rather than milk and does not add any salt. Raisins and cinnamon can be added for variety, or have him sprinkle the loaf tops with sesame, poppy or caraway seeds, or with Bakon Yeast.

When you bake bread yourself, use your own favorite recipes but avoid self-rising flour, dark rye flour, milk, and salt. You can substitute your own low-sodium milk, of course.

Quick breads (bread leavened with baking powder or baking soda) can be made using your own low-sodium baking powder or baking soda. If you remember to use half again as much baking powder you will not be able to tell the difference.

Butter (Sweet)

In Europe and among many ethnic groups on the American continent, sweet (unsalted) butter is judged best, but in the United States and Canada we tend to salt our butter—originally as a preservative and to mask rancidity. Later, as refrigeration improved, we continued to add salt simply because we had developed a taste for it.

In the eastern part of the United States sweet butter is quite readily available. In some cities you may have to look for grocers and delicatessens carrying a large number of Jewish delicacies. Since many people of the Jewish faith only use sweet butter, a deli is a good source.

In the event that you cannot find it, the low-sodium dieter can easily make sweet butter by whipping cream until it turns to butter—something that has happened to most of us accidentally at one time or another. Pack the butter into a bowl or container, cover well, and store it in the refrigerator or the freezer.

Making your own butter has come to be a cult activity with natural food aficionados and that has led to a greater availability of butter churns. They are quite inexpensive and are usually available through hardware stores, gourmet shops, or health food stores.

Buttermilk

Use 1 tablespoon of lemon juice or vinegar and fill a cup with reconstituted low-sodium milk. Stir well and let stand 5 minutes before using. The longer it stands, the thicker it becomes. See Sour Cream.

Chocolate

Most chocolates and cocoas have sodium, but not Hershey brand cocoa. You can use it in any recipe calling for cocoa and in any recipe calling for chocolate if you substitute 3 tablespoons of Hershey brand cocoa and 1 tablespoon of unsalted butter or margarine for each 1-ounce square of chocolate required.

Cottage Cheese

Thoroughly rinsing commercially available cottage cheese or ricotta cheese will rid it of most of its salt. The procedure is to place the cheese in a strainer, a sieve, or cheesecloth and totally submerge it in cold water. Lift it from the water and shake it a bit to move the curds and then repeat the process. The cheese should be submerged a total of three times for about one minute each time.

Making low-sodium cottage cheese is a simple process. All you need is:

> 1 cup low-sodium milk powder
> 7½ cups warm water (120° F.)
> ¼ cup white vinegar

Pour 1¾ cups water into a bowl and sprinkle the milk powder on the surface. Beat with a rotary beater until smooth and then blend in another 1¾ cups water. *Very* slowly add the vinegar, stirring by hand.

Let the mixture stand 15 minutes and drain the liquid curd away from the whey. Add remaining 4 cups of water to the curd, stirring well to break up the curd. Drain again. Rinse again with fresh water. (The tartness of the cheese will depend upon the rinsing; if you like it tart do not overstir while rinsing.) Place the curds in a cheesecloth, hang the cheese to drain for 30 minutes. With a fork, break the cheese into curds before serving. One tablespoon contains about 1 milligram sodium.

Fructose

Fructose is a good flavor heightener in vegetable dishes and marinades as it is approximately one and a half times sweeter than table sugar. Using less of it reduces calories. You do not add it for an overall effect of sweetness, but simply because in the absence of salt the fructose acts as a flavor enhancer and seems to sharpen the taste of the other ingredients. Add with a very light hand.

Milk and Cream

There is such a thing as low-sodium milk powder and several brands are available nationally. Featherweight Skim is marketed by the Cellu Company, as is Lonolac, a brand of powdered whole milk.

Cream does not have the sodium that milk in all of its forms does have, but you may see "sodium alginate" listed on cream cartons. This is used as a preservative and is present in only one tenth of 1 percent. However, *all* cream substitutes have sodium in their makeup, so stick to the real McCoy.

Peanut Butter

There are at least two low-sodium peanut butters available, but both are the smooth variety. You can make yours chunky style by chopping unsalted peanuts and blending them in, or use a food processor and grind peanuts to make your own peanut butter.

Salt Substitutes

Chemical salt substitutes are not recommended for cooking, but you might use them on food. When you see a product labeled LOW-SALT, it usually means that it has half the sodium of regular salt. Do not use it if you are on a very restricted low-sodium diet. "Salt substitutes" are about 97 percent potassium chloride. These products usually leave a somewhat bitter aftertaste, as mentioned in a previous chapter.

However, citrus juices and peels, vinegar, and dry table wines are excellent flavor enhancers and contain no sodium. And, angostura bitters can be used in almost any dish or beverage.

Sour Cream

Age buttermilk made by adding 1 tablespoon vinegar or lemon juice to 1 cup reconstituted low-sodium milk powder. After one week it will be thick, in three weeks even thicker, and when you pour some milk off it will be even thicker.

Syrup

Make your own from a product called Mapeline. Directions are on the back. You can boil it down to the thickness you prefer.

Thickeners

When a recipe uses egg yolk or cream for a thickener, use reconstituted low-sodium milk (see Milk and Cream) instead and thicken with flour or cornstarch.

Yogurt

With a collection of small jars, baby food containers, spice jars, custard cups, or small soufflé dishes, you can make your own yogurt. (Do not use metal containers unless they are enameled.)

You do have to begin with low-fat yogurt from a commercial source, so there will be a small amount of sodium in your homemade yogurt, but much less than in the purchased products.

> 1 quart warm water
> 2½ cups low-sodium dry milk powder
> 2 tablespoons low-fat yogurt

In a bowl add water to milk powder and stir to dissolve. Add yogurt and let stand at 90° F. to 114° F. for five to eight hours, until it sets. Refrigerate immediately so that it does not sour. You can make another batch by using 2 tablespoons of your own yogurt, but on the third batch you will need to use new commercially produced yogurt.

Yogurt-makers have become popular as they have the virtue of maintaining an even temperature. If you do not have one, cover the bowl with a lid or plate and then with a bath towel. Place the bowl over the pilot light on your range, or in a gas oven with a pilot light for the five to eight hours necessary.

CHAPTER X

ADD FLAVOR
TO THE
LOW-SODIUM DIET

Spices and herbs have little sodium content of their own, but
the flavors they bring to food can do wonders to put delicious
enjoyment back into meals where sodium has been reduced.

The average sodium content of all spices listed in the table
below is less than 1 milligram per teaspoon. As can be seen,
the majority of the spices are considerably under that, while
the highest—parsley flakes—measures not quite 6 milligrams
per teaspoon. By comparison, a teaspoon of salt contains 2,300
milligrams of sodium. To give these figures more perspective,
it is estimated that the average American consumes 10,000 to
20,000 milligrams of sodium from all food sources a day. The
government recommends we reduce this to 5,000 to 6,000 milligrams a day. Even in severely restricted sodium diets of 500
to 700 milligrams a day, the sodium contribution of spices in a
recipe is not apt to be significant.

There are many seasoning blends in addition to the spices
listed here, but some contain salt, so it is important to read
labels carefully. In all cases, be sure you calculate by the
portion, not the total recipe. For example, in the Baked Fish
Continental recipe in Chapter XI, "Low Sodium Recipes," approximately 8½ teaspoons of seasonings are used (instant
minced onion, basil, paprika, garlic powder, and parsley
flakes), yet the *per portion* contribution of sodium from all
these items combined is a little less than 3 milligrams. Even
when the daily "budget"is only 500 milligrams, a spice invest-
ment of 3 milligrams in one meal is a minuscule "price" to
pay for food enjoyment.

Table 5. SODIUM CONTENT OF SPICES

Spice	Milligrams per teaspoon	Spice	Milligrams per teaspoon
Allspice	1.4	Mustard powder	0.1
Anise seeds	0.1	Nutmeg	0.2
Basil	0.4	Onion powder	0.8
Bay leaves	0.3	Oregano	0.3
Caraway seeds	0.4	Paprika	0.4
Cardamom seeds	0.2	Parsley flakes	5.9
Celery seeds	4.1	Pepper, black	0.2
Chili powder	4.0	Pepper, chili	0.2
Cinnamon	0.2	Pepper, red	0.2
Cloves	4.2	Pepper, white	0.2
Coriander	0.3	Poppy seeds	0.2
Cumin seeds	0.3	Rosemary leaves	0.5
Curry powder, app.	1.0	Saffron	0.2
Dill seeds	0.2	Sage	0.1
Fennel seeds	1.9	Savory	0.3
Garlic powder	0.1	Sesame seeds	0.6
Ginger	0.5	Tarragon	1.0
Mace	1.3	Thyme	1.2
Marjoram	1.3	Turmeric	0.2

USES AND QUANTITIES WHEN COOKING WITH SPICES AND HERBS

Allspice

USES: Whole allspice may be used in soups; stews; pot roasts; sauerbraten; sauces; marinades; beverages; preserves; stewed fruit; and in poaching, boiling, or steaming fish or shellfish.

Use ground allspice in cakes, cookies, candy, frosting, plum pudding, fruit pies, mincemeat, and fruit. Also try it in meat loaf; pot roast; sauces such as chili, catsup, tomato, spaghetti, and barbecue sauce; French dressing; soups; and pickled eggs.

AMOUNTS (measures are for dried herbs):

Ground:

Pie crust: 1 teaspoon to 1½–2 cups graham cracker crumbs
Frosting: ¼–½ teaspoon to 1 pound confectioner's sugar

½ teaspoon to 1 cup toasted coconut for use with fruits, pudding topping or with curry dishes

Whole:

Soup: 3 in 2–3 cups pea soup
Poached fish: 4–6 to each 2 pounds fish

Anise Seeds

USES: Anise seeds may be used whole or crushed in cookies, cakes, breads, candy, applesauce, sausage, beverages, fruit pies, beef stew, fruit salads, salad dressings, appetizers, baked apples, stewed fruits, sauces and in fish and shellfish cookery.

AMOUNTS:

Crushed:

Apples: ½–1 teaspoon to 6 baked or stewed apples
Coffee cake: ¼–½ teaspoon in one 8-inch cake
Fish: ¼–½ teaspoon to 2 tablespoons unsalted butter for basting 1 pound fish

Whole:

Cupcakes: 1 tablespoon sprinkled over tops of 2 dozen cupcakes
Cookies: 1½–2 teaspoons in 5 dozen cookies

Basil

USES: Basil is sometimes called the "tomato herb" and may be used in most tomato recipes. It's also widely used when preparing stuffings, noodles, rice, venison, pork, duck, lobster, shrimp, fish, veal, lamb, green or vegetable salads, French dressing, soups, eggplant, potatoes, carrots, spinach, peas, eggs, cheese, jelly, and barbecue sauce—and it blends well with other herbs in seasoning foods.

AMOUNTS:

Spread on bread: ¼–¾ teaspoon to ½ cup unsalted butter
Vegetables: ¼–½ teaspoon to 2 cups green vegetables
Pork chops or roasts: ¾–1½ teaspoons to 1½ pounds meat
Cauliflower: ½–¾ teaspoon to 1 head
Fish or chicken: ⅛–¼ teaspoon to 2 tablespoons unsalted butter for basting 1 pound fish or 1½ pounds chicken
Eggs: ¼–½ teaspoon to 6 scrambled eggs, egg salad, or creamed eggs

Bay Leaves

USES: Bay leaves are used in soups; chowders; steaming, boiling, or poaching fish and shellfish; tomato juice; custard sauce; French dressing; marinades; water for cooking vegetables; and when preparing aspics, pot roast, sauerbraten, game, and stews.

Caraway Seeds

USES: Caraway seeds give rye bread its distinctive flavor. This spice is also used in corn bread; biscuits; waffles; rice; noodles; potatoes; cookies; baked or stewed apples; cottage cheese; seasoned butters; cake; potato, cream of pea, and corn soup; chowders; turnips; cauliflower; coleslaw; beets; green beans; carrots; zucchini; sauerkraut; cabbage; cabbage rolls; lamb stew; marinades for meats; and in preparing pork, lamb, roast goose, and guinea hen.

AMOUNTS:

Corn bread, waffles, or biscuits: 1 teaspoon–1 tablespoon to 2 cups dough mixture
Vegetables: 1 teaspoon to ¼ cup melted unsalted butter
Pork: ½–¾ teaspoon, crushed, to 1½ pounds meat
Noodles: ¼–1 teaspoon to 1 8-ounce package
Onion, meat, or vegetable pies: ½–1 teaspoon to 1 unsalted pastry crust
Potato salad: 1–2 teaspoons to 3 cups salad
Cakes: ½–1 teaspoon mixed in batter of pound or spice cake, or sprinkled over top before baking
Cucumber dressing: ½ teaspoon in vinegar or cream dressings for 2 cups sliced cucumbers

Cardamom

USES: Cardamom is a principal spice in Danish pastry. It's also used in coffee cake, sweetbreads, fruit salad dressings, fruit salads, fruit soups, fruit pies, cookies, cakes, gingerbread, curry powder, punch, grape jelly, custards, puddings, squash, hot spiced wines, barbecue sauce, rice pudding, and honey.

Amounts:

Ground:

Blueberry muffins: dash–¼ teaspoon in 12 muffins
Fruit: dash–⅛ teaspoon to 4 cups crushed strawberries, peaches, or raspberries
Meringue: ⅛–½ teaspoon to 8 egg whites for meringue shells or floating island meringues
Cake: ⅛–¼ teaspoon in 1 two-layer cake
Baked beans: dash in 2 cups beans
Toasted coconut: dash in 1 cup

Whole:

Sauerbraten: 2–4 to a 4-pound roast
Mulled wine: 2–3 in 1 quart wine
4–6 in 6 cups glögg (warm, spiced wine)
Fruit ring: 4–6 in frozen 1–1½-quart mold
Fruit punch: 6–8 in 2 gallons punch
Compote: 2–4 in 2½ cups canned or fresh fruit
Custard: 4–6 in 2 cups scalded milk

NOTE: 10 whole cardamom, shelled, seeds crushed, equal ½ teaspoon ground cardamom.

Celery Seeds

USES: Celery seeds are used in egg dishes, meat loaf, stews, soups and chowders, salad dressings, tuna or salmon salad, stewed tomatoes, canapés, dips, bread and rolls, pastries, tomato juice, tomato sauce, coleslaw, potato salad, tomato aspic, fruit salad, sandwich spreads, vegetables, croquettes, sauerkraut, clam juice, relishes, stuffings, and butters.

Amounts:

Potato salad: ⅛–¼ teaspoon in 4 cups salad
Bread: 1–2 teaspoons in 2 tablespoons unsalted butter for brushing over hot bread and rolls
Coleslaw dressing: ½–2 teaspoons in 1 cup dressing
Relish: ½–2 teaspoons to each pint
Salad dressing: 1 teaspoon to 1½ cups dressing for fruit or vegetable salads

Chili Powder

USES: Chili powder is a major ingredient in many Mexican or Mexican-style dishes such as chili con carne, tamale pie, guacamole, enchiladas, and tamales. It may also be used in sauces such as cocktail, cream, tomato, or barbecue; dips; egg dishes; gravies; stews; meat loaf; salad dressings; venison dishes; corn and cornmeal dishes; some skillet and chicken dishes; marinades for meats and poultry; seasoned, toasted bread slices; bean casseroles; eggplant; and Spanish rice.

AMOUNTS:

Corn: ¼–½ teaspoon in 2 cups cream-style corn
Guacamole: ⅛–½ teaspoon to 1 large avocado
Noodles or rice: 1–2 tablespoons to about 8 cups noodle or rice skillet dishes
Chili con carne: 2–3 tablespoons to 6 cups chili
French dressing: ¼ teaspoon to 1½ cups dressing
Pot roast: 1–2 tablespoons to 4 pounds meat

Cinnamon

USES: Whole cinnamon is used in beverages such as hot chocolate and mulled wine and as stirrers for beverages. It's also used in certain apple dishes, for stewed prunes, apricots and other dried fruits, fruit compote, in cooking some vegetables and in preserving.

Ground cinnamon is used in preparing sweetbreads, fruit soup, some vegetable and meat soups, pork, lamb roast, lamb stews, creamed chicken, hot chocolate, fruit punches and salads, plum pudding, fruitcake, apple pie and dumplings, applesauce, apple butter, baked apples, puddings, custards, squash, pumpkin pie, cookies, ice cream, French and cinnamon toast, doughnuts, cinnamon rolls, jams, preserves, chocolate fudge and dessert sauces. Sprinkle over cakes; cookies; hot cereals; eggnog; milk shakes; custards; broiled grapefruit; and rice, bread, or tapioca pudding.

AMOUNTS:

Ground:

Chocolate cake: 1–4 teaspoons in 1 two-layer cake
Chocolate pudding: ½–1 teaspoon to 2 cups milk

Vanilla pudding: ⅛–¾ teaspoon to 2 cups milk
Vanilla ice cream: 1 teaspoon to 1 quart ice cream
Apple desserts: 1 teaspoon to 2½–3 cups apples for pie, apple crisp, or stewed apples
Soup: dash–⅛ teaspoon to 1 quart chicken, tomato, or fruit soup

Whole:

Rhubarb: one 3-inch piece to 4 cups rhubarb
Fruit desserts: one or two 3-inch pieces to 3 cups stewed fruit or fruit compote
Hot beverage: one or two 3-inch pieces in 1 quart cider, tea, or coffee
Cranberries: one or two 3-inch pieces to 1 quart cranberries for pie, sauce, relish or salad
Custard sauce: one 3-inch piece to 2 cups sauce
Peaches: one 3-inch piece to each quart spiced peaches

Cloves

USES: Whole cloves are used for garnishes as well as flavor. Use to stud fruit, fruit peels, onions, or glazed pork. Use in beverages, pot roast, sauces, soups, and tomato juice.

Ground cloves are used in spice cakes, fruitcakes, gingerbread, plum pudding, cookies, some breads, fruit pies and salads, frostings, cooked fruits, meringues, glazes, mincemeat, chili sauce, catsup, tomatoes, squash, green vegetables, beverages, soups, and in combination with other spices.

AMOUNTS:

Ground:

Rhubarb: ⅛–¼ teaspoon in 4 cups rhubarb
Pork roast: ¾ teaspoon to 6 pounds meat
Mincemeat or fruit pies: dash–¼ teaspoon
Vegetables: ⅛ teaspoon to 2 cups green vegetables, squash, carrots
Jelly or jam: ¼–½ teaspoon to 8 cups blueberry, cherry, or grape jam or jelly
Cookies: ½ teaspoon in 7 dozen cookies
Fruitcake: ½–1 teaspoon in 12 to 14 pounds fruitcake

Whole:

Rice: 4–12 to 1 cup uncooked rice
Beverages: 1–2 to 1 cup hot or iced tea or mulled wine
Spiced peaches: 2–3 to each peach
Meat marinade: 6–8 in marinade for 4 pounds meat

Kaurabiedes (Greek Easter cookies): 1 in each cookie
Spiced cherries: ½–1 teaspoon to 2 cups spiced cherries

Coriander

USES: Use whole coriander seeds in punch, afterdinner coffee, and wassail bowl. The crushed seeds are used to prepare candies, cookies, gingerbread, and Danish pastry; poaching, broiling, or baking fish or chicken; making curry sauces; sausage; bean, pea, lentil, and vegetable soups; apple pie; coffee cake; sweet buns; muffins; waffles; rice pudding; bread pudding; tapioca; custards; applesauce; stewed fruits; fruit causes; lamb stew; roast pork; pork chops; stuffing for poultry and game; and meat sauces.

AMOUNTS:

Crushed:

Chicken: 2 teaspoons to 3 pounds chicken
Apple pie: ¾ teaspoon in 9- or 10-inch pie
Fish: ½–1 teaspoon to 1 pound fish
Biscuits or muffins: ¼ teaspoon in 12 biscuits or muffins
Vegetable soup: ¼ teaspoon to 1 quart soup
Vegetables: ¼ teaspoon to ¼ cup unsalted butter for 2 cups vegetables

Whole:

Coffee: 1 in each 8 ounces demitasse coffee
Meat: 6–10 in marinade for 2 pounds meat

Cumin Seeds

USES: Cumin is used commercially as a principal ingredient in both chili powder and curry powder. Cumin seeds are sometimes substituted for caraway seeds. They may be used either whole or ground in rice, chili con carne, tamales, tamale pie, eggs, soup, stew, salad dressings, tomato sauce, barbecue sauce, sauerkraut, cookies, bread, potatoes, lentils, cabbage, dried beans of all kinds, and in cooking game and wild fowl.

AMOUNTS:

Rice: ⅛–¼ teaspoon to 1 cup rice
Eggs: dash–¼ teaspoon to 6 eggs, deviled or baked Mexican style
Lamb: ¼–½ teaspoon in marinade for 1½ pounds meat

Mayonnaise: dash–⅛ teaspoon to 1 cup
Soup: dash–⅛ teaspoon to 4 cups chowder, bisque, or lentil, bean, pea or chicken soup

Curry Powder

USES: Both Indian and Madras curry powder are used to make curried lamb, fish, shrimp, lobster, rice, chicken, eggs, fruit, pork, veal, duck, sauce, soup, casseroles, and dips. Curry powder is also used as a seasoning in salad dressings, on vegetables and dried beans, in breads, and in marinades.

AMOUNTS:

Lamb: 1–3 tablespoons to 1 pound cubed lamb
Corn muffins: ½–1 teaspoon in 12 muffins
Fruit compote: 1–2 tablespoons to 6 cups mixed fruit
Eggs: ¼–½ teaspoon to 6 stuffed eggs
Curry sauce: 1–3 teaspoons to 2 cups creamy sauce
Seafood salad: ½–1 teaspoon to 2 cups salad

Dill

USES: Dill seeds are used in salads, sauerkraut, green beans, egg dishes, tomato juice, soups, sauces, stews, salad dressings, breads, butters, and in preparing fish, shellfish, and chicken.

Dill weed is used in salads, sauces, egg dishes, tomato juice, vegetables, breads, fish and shellfish recipes, cottage or cream cheese, salad dressings, noodles, rice, and may be used as a garnish.

AMOUNTS:

Dill Seed:

Cauliflower: ¼–1 teaspoon to 1 head
Vegetables: ⅛–½ teaspoon to 2 cups green vegetables
Fish, vegetables, or bread: ¼–½ teaspoon, crushed, to 2 tablespoons unsalted butter for seasoning

Dill Weed:

Cottage cheese: ⅛–1 teaspoon to 1½ cups rinsed cottage cheese
White sauce: ¼–½ teaspoon to 1 cup white sauce
Eggs: ¼–½ teaspoon to 6 stuffed eggs
Vegetables: ¼–¾ teaspoon in 2 cups vegetables

Noodles: ½–1 teaspoon to 1 8-ounce package
Chicken: ¼–½ teaspoon to 3 pounds poultry

Fennel Seeds

USES: Fennel seeds are used in egg dishes, oyster and fish dishes, cheese dishes, stews, breads, seafood salads, salad dressings, vegetables, baked or stewed apples, soups, sauerkraut, spaghetti sauce, marinades, sautéed mushrooms, cakes, cookies, and when boiling shellfish.

AMOUNTS:

Crushed:

Fish: 1–2 teaspoons to 1 pound fish
Potato salad: ⅛ teaspoon to 3 cups salad

Whole:

Vegetables: a few seeds–⅛ teaspoon in water when cooking artichokes, broccoli, Brussels sprouts, cauliflower, beans, and lentils
Pork roast: ¼–¾ teaspoon for 4 pounds meat
Mushrooms: 5–10 seeds to ½ cup sautéed mushrooms
Shrimp: ⅛–½ teaspoon for boiling 1 pound shrimp

Garlic

USES: Any of the garlic products may be increased or decreased to suit individual taste. Garlic products are excellent in tomato dishes; soups; dips; sauces; butters; gravies; salads; some vegetables; meat, poultry, or fish cookery; stews; marinades and for making garlic bread. Garlic may be used in combination with onion.

AMOUNTS:

Garlic Powder:

Meat: ⅛–¼ teaspoon to 2 pounds pork, lamb, or other meats
Bread, vegetables, and grilled meats: ⅛–½ teaspoon in ½ cup unsalted butter
Sauces: ⅛–¼ teaspoon to 3 cups tomato, barbecue, or other sauces
Soup: dash–⅛ teaspoon in 3 cups tomato or meat stock soups

NOTE: When using garlic powder in a recipe with a high acid content, a more distinctive garlic flavor may be obtained by moistening the garlic powder in water before adding. Use 2 parts water to 1 part garlic powder.

Garlic Chips:

Chicken: ⅛–½ teaspoon to 3 pounds chicken for stewing

NOTE: Use in place of fresh garlic in soups, stews, and marinades. Also garlic chips may be inserted into meats before roasting.

Instant Minced Garlic:

Salad dressing: 1½ teaspoons in 1 cup lemon oil dressing
Chutney or relish: dash–⅛ teaspoon in 2 pints chutney or relish

Ginger

USES: Whole ginger is used in syrups, stewed fruits, preserves, tea, and ginger beer. Some recipes refer to "bruised" ginger. To bruise ginger, pound to break skin but not root.

Ground ginger is one of the most versatile of all spices. Use in preparing cakes; cookies; gingerbread; ginger toast; bread; rice, bread, fruit, or steamed puddings; custards; whipped cream; sauces; soups; appetizers; Oriental dishes; lamb; pork; veal; venison; nearly all vegetables. Ginger is particularly good in preserves, conserves, baked or stewed fruits, fruit pies and salads, punch, poultry, and ice cream. It is excellent in combination with other spices.

AMOUNTS:

Pork: ¼–2 teaspoons for 1½ pounds pork
Carrots: dash–¼ teaspoon to 2 cups sliced carrots
Fruit: ¼ teaspoon to 3 cups mixed fruit
¼ teaspoon to 1 cup toasted coconut
Puddings: dash–¼ teaspoon in 4–6 servings bread or rice puddings
Cookies: 1–1½ teaspoons in 2 cups flour
Meringue: ⅛–¼ teaspoon to 2 egg whites

NOTE: Ground ginger may be used in many recipes in place of whole ginger—1 teaspoon ground ginger may be substituted for 10 to 12 pieces whole ginger about the size of shelled peanuts.

Lemon and Orange Peel

USES: Lemon and orange peel may be used in the preparation of bread or rice puddings, breads, meringue shells, tortes, waffles, shortcakes, cakes, cookies, frostings, fillings, custards, dessert soufflés, fruit pies, dried fruit, pastry, pork, chicken, duckling, seafood, dessert and meat sauces, stuffings, and most vegetables.

AMOUNTS:

Dried fruit: 1–3 teaspoons to 2 cups dried prunes or other fruits
Waffles: 4 teaspoons in 2 cups waffle recipe using 2 cups flour
Fish: ½–1 teaspoon lemon peel to 1 pound fish
Vanilla pudding: ¼–1½ teaspoons to 2 cups milk
Cake: 1½–3 teaspoons in 1 two-layer cake or an 8-inch coffee cake
Vegetables: ½–1½ teaspoons to 2 cups peas or carrots
Meat or Fowl: 1–2 teaspoons to 3 pounds pork, chicken, or duckling

Mace

USES: Mace has a variety of uses and can be substituted for nutmeg in recipes. Use mace in preparing pork; lamb; chicken; fish; pound, spice, and devil's food cake; gingerbread; frosting; hot chocolate; puddings; custards; fruit, chiffon, custard, or refrigerator pie; breads; soups; punches; apple dishes; sauces; creamed dishes; waffles; pancakes; doughnuts; coffee cakes; Danish pastries; glazes; muffins; vegetables; fruit salads; fruit salad dressings.

AMOUNTS:

Muffins: dash–½ teaspoon in 12 muffins
Chocolate pudding or cake: ⅛–¼ teaspoon to 2 cups milk for pudding, or in two-layer cake
Dried apricots: ¼ teaspoon to 2 cups dried apricots for stewing
Coffee cake: ⅛–¼ teaspoon in one 8-inch cake
Waffles: 1 teaspoon to 2 cups flour
Spinach: dash to 1 package frozen spinach, or about 1 cup fresh cooked spinach
Chicken or tuna: dash–⅛ teaspoon to 4 cups creamed chicken or tuna
White sauce: dash–⅛ teaspoon to 2 cups white sauce
Glaze: ⅛–¼ teaspoon in 2 cups confectioners' sugar
Cake: ⅛–¼ teaspoon in pound cake

Marjoram

USES: Marjoram is used in the preparation of lamb; pork; veal; venison and other game; chicken; broiled or baked fish; shellfish; practically all tomato dishes; other vegetables such as carrots, cauliflower, peas, spinach, squash, mushrooms, beans, broccoli and Brussels sprouts; spaghetti and brown sauces; stuffings; egg dishes; breads; tossed green salads; and salad dressings.

AMOUNTS:

Green vegetables: ½–1 teaspoon to 2 cups green vegetables
Chicken: ¼–½ teaspoon to 3 pounds chicken
Pork: ⅛–½ teaspoon to 1½ pounds pork
Veal: ¼–½ teaspoon for 1 pound veal
Eggs: dash–¼ teaspoon to 4 scrambled or stuffed eggs, or eggs for omelettes
Carrots: ½ teaspoon to 2 cups carrots
Tomato sauce: dash–¼ teaspoon to 2 cups sauce
Stuffing: ¼ teaspoon to 3 cups bread cubes

Mint

USES: Use in lamb stew and on lamb roast, vegetables, sauces for lamb, mint jelly, syrups, fruit compotes, fruit soup, split pea soup, devil's food cake, frostings, ice cream and sherbet, chocolate pudding, custards, candies, hot chocolate, punches, tea, and sauces for desserts.

AMOUNTS (MINT FLAKES):

Crushed:

Chocolate pudding: ¼–½ teaspoon to about 2 cups milk
White cake: ¼–1 teaspoon in 1 two-layer cake
Chocolate cake: ½–1½ teaspoons in 1 two-layer cake
Peas: ¼–1 teaspoon to 2 cups peas

Whole:

Lamb stew: ¼ teaspoon to 1–1½ pounds meat
Fruit: ¼–1 teaspoon to 3–4 cups fruit
Beverages: ½ teaspoon to 1 quart tea or fruit beverages

Mustard

USES: Mustard seeds are used in preparing cucumbers, vegetable relishes, corned beef, boiled beef, coleslaw, potato salad, boiled cabbage, and sauerkraut. Dry mustard adds zip to egg dishes, salad dressings, appetizers, meats, poultry, sauces, and vegetables.

AMOUNTS (DRY MUSTARD):

Eggs: ¼–½ teaspoon to 6 stuffed or scrambled eggs, or for omelettes
Mustard sauce: ½–1 teaspoon to 1 teaspoon vinegar and dash turmeric for 2 teaspoons mustard sauce (hotter than commercial prepared mustard)

Nutmeg

USES: Ground nutmeg or the freshly grated whole nutmeg may be sprinkled over hot and cold milk drinks, eggnog, fruits, puddings, and soups and is used to season meats, poultry, seafood, vegetables, and sauces. Use in making cakes, cookies, doughnuts, pies, pastries, muffins, waffles, and coffee cakes.

AMOUNTS:

Layer cake: ¼–½ teaspoon in 1 two-layer white or yellow cake
Pastry: ½–1 teaspoon for 1 two-crust pastry
Vegetables: dash–¼ teaspoon to 2 cups spinach, mixed vegetables, sliced carrots, or most other vegetables
Vanilla pudding: ⅛–¾ teaspoon to about 2 cups milk
Muffins, coffee cakes, and waffles: ¼ teaspoon to about 2 cups batter
Frosting: ½ teaspoon in chocolate frosting for two cake layers
Glaze: ⅛–¼ teaspoon to 1 cup whipped heavy cream, or 1 cup confectioners' sugar
Chicken or tuna: dash–⅛ teaspoon to 4 cups creamed chicken or tuna
Pound cake: ¼–½ teaspoon in pound cake

NOTE: One whole nutmeg, grated, equals 2 to 3 teaspoons ground nutmeg.

Onion

USES: Onion products may be used in the preparation of appetizers and dips, soups and chowders, stews, meats, game, fish, shellfish, poultry, salads and salad dressings, sauces, vegetables, gravies, stuffings, egg dishes, breads, casseroles, croquettes and rice dishes.

AMOUNTS:

Onion Powder:

Vegetables: ¼–1 teaspoon to 2 cups vegetables
Spreads: 1 teaspoon to 1 pound cooked meat for spreads

NOTE: When using onion powder in a recipe with an extremely high acid content, a more distinctive onion flavor may be obtained by moistening onion powder in water before adding to the recipe; use 2 parts water to 1 part onion powder.

Onion Salt:

Vegetables: 1–2 teaspoons in 2 cups vegetables
Meat and poultry: ¼–1 teaspoon to 1 pound chicken, stew meat, veal, variety meats, game, roasts, or chops

Instant Minced Onion:

Salad dressing: ½–1½ teaspoons to 1 cup lemon oil dressing
Beans: 1–2 tablespoons to 1 pound dried beans
Vegetables: 1–2 teaspoons to 2 cups vegetables
Meat: 2–3 teaspoons to 1 pound lamb or veal
Tuna: 1–3 teaspoons to 7-ounce can tuna

Onion Flakes:

Soup: 1 tablespoon to 4 cups soup

Chopped Instant Onions:

Soup: ¼ cup in 6 cups chowder, or chicken or vegetable soup

NOTE: Particularly good as sautéed onions for French onion soup or with liver. Reconstitute in ice water for use in salads.

Shredded Green Onions:

Eggs: ½–1 teaspoon to 6 creamed or scrambled eggs, or eggs for omelettes
Corn: 1–2 teaspoons to 2 cups corn, sautéed or in casserole
Rice or noodles: 1 tablespoon to 1 cup rice or noodles

NOTE: May be used as a garnish.

Onion Juice: Use onion juice when a mild flavor of onion is desired. It combines well with other ingredients giving an even overall hint of onion.

Oregano

USES: Oregano goes well with tomatoes and is a natural seasoning with any tomato dish. Use to season pasta sauces, tomato juice, chili con carne, barbecue sauce, and vegetable soup. It is excellent in egg dishes; seafood salads; stuffings for meat or poultry; sauce for fish; with onions; and on pork, lamb, chicken, and fish.

AMOUNTS:

Ground:

Pork: ¼–½ teaspoon to 1 pound meat

Leaves:

Egg salad: ¼–¾ teaspoon to 4 eggs
Baked potatoes, bread, or fish: ¼–½ teaspoon to ½ cup unsalted butter
Vegetables: ¼–½ teaspoon to 2 cups spinach or green beans, or 3 cups tomatoes
Bread: 1 teaspoon to 3 cups flour in yeast bread
Sauces: ⅛–¼ teaspoon to 2 cups tomato, spaghetti, or barbecue sauce (ground oregano may also be used)

Paprika

USES: Use as a colorful garnish for any light-color food. Sprinkle on fish, meats, canapés, soups, potatoes, eggs, and sauces. Used in generous quantities, paprika is the principal seasoning in such dishes as Hungarian goulash and chicken or veal paprikash and is often used in making French dressing.

AMOUNTS:

Chicken or meat: ½ teaspoon–2 tablespoons in flour for dredging 3 pounds chicken or meat
French dressing: ¼–¾ teaspoon to 1 cup vinegar and oil
Potatoes, vegetables: ½ teaspoon to ¼ cup unsalted butter for sautéing potatoes or to season white vegetables
Veal: 1 teaspoon–1 tablespoon to 2 pounds veal in veal paprikash

Parsley

USES: Garnish and flavor broiled or fried fish, meats, poultry, canapés, soups, tossed green salads, coleslaw, breads, herb sauces, butters, tomato and meat sauces, stuffings for fish and meat.

AMOUNTS:

Noodles or rice: 2–4 teaspoons to one 8-ounce package noodles or 3 cups cooked rice
Tomato sauce: 1–2 teaspoons to 2–3 cups sauce

Vegetables, fish, or meats: ½–1 teaspoon to ½ cup unsalted butter
Eggs: ¼–1 teaspoon to 2 scrambled eggs or eggs for omelette

Pepper

USES: Peppercorns or whole black peppers are used in pepper mills. Grind the pepper over foods at the table or when food is being prepared. Peppercorns are also used in some salad dressings, in marinades, poached fish, soups, sauces, and stews.

Ground white pepper is especially popular in white or light-color foods where the dark specks of black pepper do not add to the aesthetic appearance. White pepper may be substituted for black pepper in any recipe.

Black pepper comes in three different grinds: fine, coarse, and cracked. It may be used in any dish except sweets. However, it is sometimes used in cake and is a characteristic ingredient in the German Christmas cookie, pfeffernusse.

AMOUNTS:

Peppercorns:

Fish: 4–6 in liquid for poaching 1–2 pounds fish
Chicken and shrimp: 8–10 in liquid when boiling 5 pounds chicken or shrimp

Ground Black Pepper:

Spice cake: ⅛–½ teaspoon in spice cake
Tuna salad: ⅛–½ teaspoon to a 7-ounce can tuna
Pfeffernusse: ¼–½ teaspoon in 6 dozen cookies

Coarse Grind Black Pepper:

Dressings: ¼–½ teaspoon to 1½ cups French or other salad dressings
Stuffings: ⅛–½ teaspoon to 4 cups bread cubes
Meat, fish, poultry: ⅛–¼ teaspoon sprinkled over 1 pound chops, fish, chicken, or liver before broiling

Cracked Black Pepper:

Salad: ⅛ teaspoon to each individual salad bowl of chef's or tossed salad
Eggs: dash–⅛ teaspoon to 6 stuffed, scrambled, or creamed eggs, or eggs for omelettes
Mashed potatoes: ⅛–¼ teaspoon to 2 cups mashed potatoes
Sauce: ¼ teaspoon to 2 cups white or light-color sauce

Soups: ⅛–¼ teaspoon to 2 cups vichyssoise or other light-color soups
Fish: ⅛–¼ teaspoon for 1 pound fish
Cauliflower: ⅛–¼ teaspoon for 1 head

Pepper, Red

USES: Both cayenne and red pepper are widely used in Mexican and Italian dishes. Use to season meats, seafood, poultry, game, deviled eggs, appetizers, soups and chowders, tomato aspic, cottage and cream cheese, sauces, gravies, salad dressings, vegetables, creamed dishes, seviche, dips, spread for canapés, tomato juice cocktail, Bloody Marys, omelettes, soufflés, croquettes, tamale pie, and guacamole.

Crushed red pepper is particularly important in chowders, gumbos, spaghetti sauce, and in making sausage.

AMOUNTS:

Cayenne and Red Pepper:

Shrimp: dash–¼ teaspoon to 1 pound shrimp
Eggs: dash–⅛ teaspoon to 6 stuffed or scrambled eggs, or eggs for omelettes
Chicken, fish, vegetables: dash–⅛ teaspoon to ½ cup unsalted butter for basting chicken or fish, or to use over vegetables

Crushed Red Pepper:

Spaghetti sauce: ⅛–¼ teaspoon to 2 cups sauce
Tomato relish and green beans: 1–2 teaspoons to 4 pints tomato relish or dilled green beans

NOTE: A good rule to follow is to use a dash to ⅛ teaspoon in most recipes for four servings unless extremely hot food is desired. Increase to suit individual taste.

Pickling Spice

USES: Pickling spice may be used in stewed prunes, marinades, sauerbraten, spiced fruits, boiled shrimp, and game cookery.

AMOUNTS:

Prunes: 1–2 teaspoons to 2 cups prunes for stewing
Beets: 1 teaspoon–1 tablespoon to 2 cups whole beets
Fruit: 1 tablespoon to 4 cups mixed fruits or fruit cocktail

Shrimp: 2–4 tablespoons to 1 quart water for boiling 1–2 pounds shrimp

Venison: 1–2 tablespoons to 4 pounds meat

Poppy Seeds

USES: Poppy seeds may be used as an ingredient in a recipe, sprinkled over the top of food before cooking, or as a garnish. Use in rinsed cottage cheese, scrambled eggs, pie crust, fruit compotes, fruit salad dressings, cookies, cakes, breads, and noodles. Sprinkle over top of fruit salads, vegetables, breads, cookies, cakes, and casseroles.

AMOUNTS:

Muffins: 1–3 teaspoons in 12 corn or plain muffins
Pastry: 2–4 teaspoons in a two-crust pastry
Noodles: ½–1 teaspoon to ½ cup unsalted butter and stir into 8-ounce package, cooked
Fruit salad dressing: 1 teaspoon to 1 cup dressing
Cake: ¼–⅓ cup in a two-layer white cake
Cookies: 2–4 tablespoons to 3 cups flour

Poultry Seasoning

USES: Poultry seasoning may be used in stuffings; roasting, broiling, or frying chicken; creamed chicken; roasting turkey; chicken, turkey, or salmon croquettes; sautéed chicken livers; chicken soups; chicken and dumplings; chicken pot pie; veal dishes; pastry for meat pies; and waffles, biscuits, and gravies.

AMOUNTS:

Frying chicken: ¼–¾ teaspoon to 3 pounds frying chicken
Chicken or turkey: ½ teaspoon to about 4 cups creamed chicken or turkey
Stuffing: ½–2 teaspoons to 4 cups bread cubes
Veal: ⅛–¼ teaspoon for 1 pound meat

Pumpkin Pie Spice

USES: Pumpkin pie spice is just right for seasoning pumpkin pie. It's excellent used in gingerbread, cookies, fruits, squash, applesauce and other apple dishes, sweet rolls, frostings, waffles, muffins, whipped cream, glazes, cakes, puddings, dessert sauces, and for making toast.

AMOUNTS:

Cake: ¼–1 teaspoon in pound cake
Coconut: ¼–1 teaspoon to 1 cup flake or shredded, toasted coconut
Pie: 2–3 teaspoons to 1½ cups mashed pumpkin
Rice pudding: ½ teaspoon to ½ cup uncooked rice
Apricots: ½–1 teaspoon to 2 cups apricots for stewing, tarts, or pie

Rosemary Leaves

USES: Rosemary leaves, a sweet, fragrant herb, is excellent in lamb dishes, soups, stews, poached or boiled fish or seafood, Italian tomato sauce for fish, liver pâté, boiled potatoes, mushrooms, fruits, fruit juices, cauliflower, turnips, and breads and it is used in preparing poultry, veal, pork, wild fowl, and venison. Sprinkle rosemary over coals when barbecuing meats.

AMOUNTS:

Crushed:

Muffins and biscuits: ½–1 teaspoon in 12 corn muffins or biscuits
Lamb: ½ teaspoon to 3–4 pounds lamb roast and in combination with thyme and sage on roast

Leaves:

Chicken: ¼ teaspoon–1 tablespoon to 3 pounds chicken
Fruit: ¼ teaspoon to 4 cups mixed fruit or 2 cups fruit juice
Potatoes and vegetables: ¼–½ teaspoon to 2 cups potatoes, cauliflower, or tomatoes
Barbecue sauce: ¼ teaspoon–1 tablespoon to 6 cups sauce

Saffron

USES: Saffron is widely used in French, Spanish, and South American dishes. An essential ingredient in arroz con pollo, bouillabaisse, paella, and risotto. Saffron may also be used in chicken and seafood dishes, yeast breads, rice, soups, sauces, and cakes. The individual pieces of saffron may be used in recipes; however, it is usually crushed before using.

Crushed:

Rice: dash–¼ teaspoon to 1 cup uncooked rice
Chicken: dash–⅛ teaspoon to 3 pounds chicken
Cake: 8–10 individual pieces in 8- or 9-inch two-layer cake
Veal: dash–⅛ teaspoon to 2 pounds veal

Whole:

Breads or buns: ⅛–1 teaspoon to 4 cups flour

Sage

USES: Sage is well-known for its use in stuffings for poultry, fish, game, and other meats. Thousands of pounds go into the commercial making of sausage each year. Sage may also be used in soups, chowders, waffles, biscuits, lima beans, saltimbocca, onions, eggplant, sauces, tomatoes, cheese, marinades, potatoes, and in preparing poultry, fish, pork, and veal.

AMOUNTS:

Vegetables: ¼–½ teaspoon to 2 cups green vegetables
Stuffing: ¼–¾ teaspoon to 1 quart bread cubes for poultry, fish, pork chops, breast of veal, and crown roasts
Barbecue sauce: ¼ teaspoon–1 tablespoon to 6 cups sauce in combination with rosemary and thyme
Waffles: 2 teaspoons to 2 cups flour
Meats: ½ teaspoon to 3 pounds pork, veal, lamb, and other meats
Lamb: ¼–½ teaspoon in 1 pound ground lamb
Soups: dash–¼ teaspoon to 3 cups cream, chowder, vegetable, tomato, or seafood soup
Dredging meat: ½ teaspoon to ¼ cup flour
Fish: dash–¼ teaspoon to ¼ cup unsalted butter for basting 1 pound fish when baking or broiling
Tomatoes: dash–¼ teaspoon to 3 cups tomatoes

Savory

USES: Savory blends well with other herbs. It may be used alone or in combination with other herbs in stuffings for meat, fish, or poultry; egg dishes; sauces; soups; stews; beans; cabbage; peas; and tomato juice.

Vegetables: ¼–½ teaspoon to 2 cups green beans, Brussels sprouts, peas, or other vegetables

Soup: dash–¼ teaspoon to 3 cups consommé; fish chowder; or bean, split pea, tomato, or vegetable soup

Stuffing: ¼ teaspoon to 3 cups bread cubes

Eggs: ⅛ teaspoon to 6 stuffed eggs

Chicken: ¼–½ teaspoon to 3 pounds chicken

Fish: ¼ teaspoon to 1 pound of fish

Sauce or gravy: dash–¼ teaspoon to 1½ cups brown sauce or gravy

Sesame Seeds

USES: The flavor of toasted sesame seeds resembles that of toasted almonds. Use, toasted or untoasted, in many of the same ways nuts are used. Sprinkle canapés, breads, cookies, casseroles, salads, noodles, soups, and vegetables with sesame seeds. Add to salt-free pie crust and fillings, candy, cakes, cookies, dumplings, cheese spreads and dips, and stuffings. When recipe calls for "toasted" seed, toast sesame seeds in 350° F. oven 15 minutes or until lightly browned before using.

AMOUNTS (TOASTED):

Dumplings: 1–2 teaspoons to 1½ cups flour

Vegetables: 1 teaspoon–1 tablespoon to 2 tablespoons melted unsalted butter for vegetables

Pastry: 2–4 tablespoons for two-crust pastry

Stuffing: ⅓ cup to 3 cups bread stuffing for poultry or pork chops

Pie: ¼ cup in pecan pie filling

NOTE: Sprinkle over waffles, biscuits, muffins, and rolls before baking.

Tarragon

USES: Tarragon is the distinctive flavor in Béarnaise sauce. This spice may be used in mayonnaise; tartar and mustard sauces; turtle soup; tuna salads and casseroles; ragouts. Use in preparing veal, lamb, venison and other game, chicken, duck, Cornish hens, squab, pheasant, fish, shellfish, and egg dishes. Excellent sprinkled over salad greens.

AMOUNTS:

Vegetables: ¼–½ teaspoon to 2 cups peas or spinach
Soup: ¼ teaspoon to 2 cups turtle, tomato, or mushroom soup, or fish chowders
Seafood: ½–1 teaspoon to ½ cup unsalted butter for sautéing shellfish or as a sauce for fish
Veal: ¼–½ teaspoon to 2 pounds veal
White sauce: ¼–½ teaspoon to 2 cups white sauce for creamed eggs or fish dishes
Fish: ¼ teaspoon to 1 pound broiled or baked fish
Salad dressing: 1 tablespoon to 3 cups mayonnaise for green goddess salad dressing
Chicken: 1 teaspoon to 3 pounds chicken
Béarnaise sauce: 1½ teaspoons to 3 egg yolks
Chops: ½–1 teaspoon to ½ cup unsalted butter for topping chops
Tarragon vinegar: 1 tablespoon to 1 pint white wine vinegar (let stand before using)

Thyme

USES: Thyme is one of the most popular herbs, and is used to season meat, poultry, and fish. Combine thyme with melted unsalted butter and serve over vegetables or broiled seafood or use in stuffing for fish and meats. Add to dishes made with tomato or cheese. Seasoning clam chowder with thyme is a must. Thyme is used in making a *bouquet garni*.

AMOUNTS:

Ground:

Chicken: ¼–½ teaspoon in flour for dredging 3 pounds chicken
Chowder: dash–½ teaspoon to 3 cups clam chowder
Lamb: ½–1¼ teaspoons to 4 pounds leg of lamb—alone or in combination with sage and rosemary
Biscuits: ¼–½ teaspoon in 12 biscuits
Barbecue sauce: ¼ teaspoon–1 tablespoon to 6 cups sauce

Leaves:

Liver: ¼–½ teaspoon for 1 pound liver
Vegetables: dash–¼ teaspoon to 2 cups Brussels sprouts or green beans
Steak: ¼–½ teaspoon to 1½ pounds round steak
Chicken: ¼–½ teaspoon to 5 pounds stewing chicken

Turmeric

USES: Turmeric is used in egg and rice dishes, cream sauces, salad dressings, breads, relish, mayonnaise, soups, noodles, and in preparing chicken and fish.

AMOUNTS:

Eggs: dash–⅛ teaspoon to 6 stuffed or scrambled eggs
Rice or noodles: dash–¼ teaspoon to 1 cup uncooked rice or 1 8-ounce package noodles
White sauce: dash–¼ teaspoon to 2 cups sauce
Chicken and seafood: ⅛–¼ teaspoon to ½ cup unsalted butter for basting chicken and seafood when broiling or baking

Vanilla

USES: Use vanilla to flavor most sweet foods such as eggnog, milk shakes, hot chocolate, and other milk beverages; ice cream; rice, bread, and other puddings; cakes; cookies; dessert or fruit sauces; custards; stewed fruits; fruit compotes; candies; glazes; frostings; whipped cream; pies; coffee; tortes; meringue shells; cheesecake; dessert soufflés; sundae toppings; cream puff and unsalted pastry fillings; muffins; coffee cakes; and cream cheese filling for fruit bread.

AMOUNTS:

Cake: 1–2 teaspoons in 1 two-layer cake
Whipped cream: ¼–½ teaspoon to 1 cup whipped heavy cream
Custard sauce: 1–1½ teaspoons to 2 cups custard sauce
Frosting: 1–1½ teaspoons in frostings for 1 two-layer cake
Cookies: 2–3 teaspoons in 5 dozen cookies
Candy: ½–1 teaspoon to 2 cups sugar
Ice cream: 2 teaspoons to about 4 cups custard for making ice cream

These items are merely a sampling of the many, many spices, herbs, and blends available to you. After reading this section and trying the suggestions it contains, we hope you will be encouraged by the evident ease of spice and herb cookery to experiment with the many other seasonings, equally popular and useful in food preparation, which have not been mentioned here because of space limitations. Some of these are: gumbo file, Italian seasoning, powdered mushrooms, charcoal seasoning, salad herbs, bell pepper flakes, vegetable flakes, chives, and arrowroot.

CHAPTER XI

LOW-SODIUM RECIPES

Once you get the hang of flavoring *sans* sodium you can convert your own recipes, but as mentioned earlier, you shouldn't begin that way. Later you can go back to favorite dishes that you are accustomed to enjoying with salt, and adapt them to a low-sodium diet. Meanwhile, try the new low-sodium recipes in this chapter. Note that they rely on herbs, wine, spirits (such as bourbon, Scotch, brandy, liqueurs), lemon and lime juice or rind, for their flavor. The alcohol evaporates if the dish is cooked. You will find flavor affinities by following your nose when making a favorite recipe. If Scotch smells like it would taste good in lamb stew, it probably would. Add just a little and taste your way along. A bonus in cooking with liqueurs such as chartreuse or vermouth is that a few drops may contain the essences of as many as 150 herbs—and that is a lot of flavor.

Flavoring ingredients such as Worcestershire sauce have some sodium, but you use so little of it per serving that the amount is negligible when figuring your daily allowance. Lea & Perrins Worcestershire sauce has only 55 milligrams of sodium per teaspoon (a teaspoon of salt has 2,300 milligrams and a teaspoon of soy sauce 365 milligrams). In most recipes the average amount of sodium from Worcestershire sauce is about 20 milligrams. Other no- or low-sodium flavoring ingredients are Tabasco and other "hot" sauces.

We hope these recipes will be helpful. Eating is too important a part of our lives to let it become a bore or a chore.

 **SOUPS**

HEARTY MEATBALL AND VEGETABLE SOUP ·
POTATO CHEDDAR CHOWDER · *SPLIT PEA SOUP*
· *VEGETABLE-BEEF SOUP* · *ZUCCHINI SOUP*

HEARTY MEATBALL AND VEGETABLE SOUP

Add leftover vegetables at will.

2 tablespoons onion flakes, or ⅓ cup chopped onion
½ teaspoon instant minced garlic, or 2 garlic cloves, minced
2½ cups plus 2 tablespoons water
1 pound lean ground beef
1½ teaspoons crushed marjoram leaves
2 tablespoons vegetable oil

1 tablespoon cider vinegar
6 whole cloves
½ teaspoon crushed thyme leaves
⅛ teaspoon ground black pepper
1 cup peeled, diced potato
2 cups shredded cabbage
1 cup diced tomato
1 tablespoon parsley flakes

Combine onion flakes and minced garlic with 2 tablespoons water; let stand for 10 minutes to soften; set aside. Mix beef with ½ teaspoon of the marjoram; shape into ½-inch balls.

In a medium saucepan heat oil. Add meatballs a few at a time; brown on all sides; remove and set aside. Add onion and garlic; sauté for 2 minutes. Add 2½ cups water, vinegar, cloves, thyme, black pepper, and remaining 1 teaspoon marjoram. Bring to the boiling point, stirring to scrape drippings from the bottom of the pan.

Return meatballs to pan. Add potato; reduce heat and simmer, covered, for 10 minutes. Add cabbage and tomato. Return to the boiling point. Reduce heat and simmer, covered, until vegetables are tender, about 10 minutes. Serve sprinkled with parsley flakes. Makes 5 cups.

POTATO CHEDDAR CHOWDER

A satisfying meatless dish.

2 cups (1 pound) diced
   potatoes
¼ cup chopped onion
2 cups boiling water
¼ cup sweet (unsalted)
   butter or margarine
¼ cup flour

2 cups reconstituted low-
   sodium milk
2 cups grated low-sodium
   sharp cheese
2½ teaspoons Worcestershire
   sauce
Paprika (optional)

In a medium saucepan combine potatoes, onion, and water. Simmer, covered, for 10 minutes; set aside (do not drain).

In another medium saucepan melt butter or margarine. Stir in flour until smooth. Gradually add milk; blend until smooth. Simmer, stirring constantly, until thickened. Remove from heat.

Add cheese; stir until cheese melts. Add undrained vegetables and Worcestershire sauce. Heat; *do not boil.* Sprinkle with paprika, if desired. Makes 5 cups.

SPLIT PEA SOUP

Free from everything but calories.

2 cups dried split peas
2 quarts water
2 meaty beef neck bones
2 onions, diced
2 carrots, scraped and finely
   diced

2 stalks celery, finely diced
Several parsley sprigs,
   minced
Several dill sprigs, minced
¾ teaspoon dill weed
¼ teaspoon pepper

Combine all ingredients in a heavy pan and bring to a boil. Lower heat, cover, and simmer 2½ to 3 hours, stirring occasionally.

To serve, remove bones and run soup through a food processor, if smooth soup is desired. Or serve as is with a bit of meat from the bones. Makes 8 portions.

VEGETABLE-BEEF SOUP

A real end-of-the-garden soup.

1 teaspoon vegetable oil
½ cup chopped onion
1 teaspoon minced garlic
9 cups water
4 cups (3 pounds) fresh peeled, chopped tomatoes
1½ pounds beef shank bones with meat attached, or short ribs

2 cups fresh sliced zucchini
2 cups cabbage, cut in 1-inch chunks
1½ cups diced potatoes
1 cup sliced carrots
1 cup small macaroni shells
1½ teaspoons crushed oregano leaves

In a large saucepan heat oil until hot. Add onion and garlic; sauté until tender, about 2 minutes. Add 6 cups water, tomatoes, and beef; bring to a boil. Reduce heat and simmer, covered, until meat is tender, about 1½ hours.

Trim meat from bones and cut into ½-inch pieces. Skim off fat from liquid. Return meat to saucepan; discard bones. Add zucchini, cabbage, potatoes, carrots, macaroni, and 3 cups water; simmer, covered, for 20 minutes. Add oregano; continue to simmer, covered, until vegetables are tender, about 10 minutes. Makes 10 portions.

ZUCCHINI SOUP

A food processor or grinder speeds up the process.

4 cups grated zucchini
½ cup water
½ teaspoon sugar
2 or more tablespoons chopped onion
2 tablespoons unsalted butter or margarine

2 tablespoons flour
2 cups reconstituted low-sodium dry milk
Freshly ground pepper to taste

Combine zucchini, water, sugar, and onion; cover and cook over low heat for 15 minutes, stirring often.

Add butter or margarine combined with flour and add the milk. Bring to a boil, stirring often. Season with fresh ground pepper and cook until starchy flavor is gone. If you prefer a thicker soup add more flour. Makes 6 portions.

 # SALADS AND DRESSINGS

SALADS *CITRUS AND ONION SALAD · CUCUMBER RAITA · MARINATED MUSHROOM SALAD · RAW CAULIFLOWER SALAD*

CITRUS AND ONION SALAD

Fresh fruit or fruits canned in their own juice can be used.

2 oranges, peeled and thinly sliced
2 grapefruit, peeled and thinly sliced
1 red onion, thinly sliced
¼ cup fresh lime juice
¼ teaspoon angostura bitters
1 tablespoon fresh chopped dill, or 1 teaspoon dried dill weed

Layer orange slices, grapefruit slices, and red onion in a bowl, sprinkling each layer with lime juice combined with bitters and dill. Let stand for 1 hour before serving. Makes 6 to 8 portions.

NOTE: To peel oranges and grapefruit, slice away all of the white membrane and then remove sections by cutting down next to the membrane separating the layers and bringing knife up on the other side of the section. Squeeze any juice from the pulp into the lime juice.

CUCUMBER RAITA

A refreshing salad.

1 large cucumber
1 cup plain yogurt
1 teaspoon lemon or lime
  juice
¼ teaspoon ground cumin
¼ teaspoon ground ginger

¼ teaspoon ground
  coriander
¼ teaspoon caraway seeds
Dash ground black pepper
Lettuce leaves

Peel and thinly slice cucumber (makes about 2 cups); set aside.

In a medium bowl combine yogurt, lemon or lime juice, cumin, ginger, coriander, caraway, and black pepper. Stir in reserved cucumber. Cover and refrigerate 1 hour.

To serve, line a serving bowl with lettuce leaves. Spoon in cucumber mixture. Garnish with a cucumber twist, if desired. Makes 4 to 6 portions (3 cups).

MARINATED MUSHROOM SALAD

Mushrooms can be sliced with an egg slicer.

1 pound fresh mushrooms
1 cup white vinegar
2 cups water
½ cup sliced carrots
½ cup diced celery
½ cup julienned green
  pepper

½ cup julienned red pepper
⅓ cup olive oil
1 teaspoon crushed oregano
  leaves
2 garlic cloves, minced
¼ teaspoon ground black
  pepper

Rinse, pat dry, and slice mushrooms (makes about 5 cups).

In a medium saucepan combine mushrooms and vinegar; bring to a boil. Reduce heat and simmer, covered, for 2 minutes. Drain mushrooms; set aside to cool.

In a small saucepan bring water to a boil. Add carrots and celery; return to a boil. Reduce heat and simmer, covered, for 3 minutes. Add red and green pepper strips; cover and simmer until all vegetables are tender, about 3 minutes. Drain and set aside to cool.

In a medium bowl mix olive oil, oregano, garlic, and black pepper. Let stand for 10 minutes.

Stir in vegetable mixture and toss well. Cover and refrigerate at least 2 hours before serving. Makes 4 to 5 portions (4½ cups).

RAW CAULIFLOWER SALAD

Chill 1 hour before serving.

1 medium head cauliflower	½ teaspoon dry mustard
1 head romaine lettuce	pepper to taste
4 shallots, minced	½ cup finely chopped
2 tablespoons wine vinegar	parsley
4 tablespoons olive oil	

Drop flowerets into a food processor one at a time to slice. Heap into bowl lined with leaves of romaine.

Combine remaining ingredients and pour over cauliflower. Makes 8 to 10 portions.

DRESSINGS *BASIC FRENCH DRESSING · FRENCH-STYLE DRESSING · ITALIAN DRESSING · RUBY RED DRESSING · SALAD SEASONING BLEND · SEEDED SALAD DRESSING · SPANISH DRESSING*

BASIC FRENCH DRESSING (Vinaigrette Française)

1 tablespoon dry mustard	1 teaspoon dill weed
1 cup red or white wine vinegar	1 teaspoon pepper
3 cups vegetable oil	1 teaspoon sugar

In a bowl mix mustard and vinegar thoroughly. Beat in oil. Season with dill weed and pepper. Add sugar to taste if vinegar is too sour. Makes 1 quart.

FRENCH-STYLE DRESSING

Can also be used as a marinade for meats and vegetables.

1 cup low-sodium catsup
1 cup vegetable oil
¾ cup granulated sugar
Juice of 1 fresh lemon
1 small onion, grated
½ teaspoon freshly ground pepper
1 cup cider vinegar

In a bottle combine all ingredients but vinegar and shake well. Add the vinegar, shake vigorously, and refrigerate. Shake before each use. Makes 3 cups.

ITALIAN DRESSING (Vinaigrette Italienne)

1 garlic clove, peeled
1 tablespoon finely chopped parsley
1 tablespoon low-sodium tomato puree
1 cup Basic French Dressing (see recipe, page 85)
Oregano to taste
Pepper to taste

Press garlic and mix with parsley. Add tomato puree and mix well. Fold in Basic French Dressing and season to taste. Makes 1 cup.

RUBY RED DRESSING

Serve over salad greens, chopped cabbage, or fruit.

2 tablespoons flour
1½ teaspoons sugar
1 teaspoon paprika
1 teaspoon powdered mustard
Pinch ground red pepper
⅔ cup water
1 egg yolk
2 tablespoons vegetable oil
2 tablespoons cider vinegar

In the top portion of a double boiler combine flour, sugar, paprika, mustard, and red pepper. Add water and egg yolk; whisk until smooth. Cook and stir over simmering water until thickened, about 5 minutes. Remove from heat.

Whisk in oil and then vinegar until smooth. Cover and chill. Makes 1 cup.

SALAD SEASONING BLEND

A high-flavor seasoning for salad dressing, sliced tomatoes, cottage cheese, vegetables, or hard-cooked eggs.

⅓ cup toasted sesame seeds*
4½ tablespoons onion powder
2 tablespoons poppy seeds
1½ tablespoons garlic powder

1½ tablespoons paprika
¾ teaspoon celery seeds
¼ teaspoon ground black pepper

Combine all ingredients in a bowl. Spoon into shaker or tightly covered container. Sprinkle over greens, sliced tomatoes, cold vegetables, cottage cheese, etc. Makes about 1 cup.

*To toast sesame seeds, place in a skillet, cook and stir over medium heat until golden, 3 to 5 minutes.

SEEDED SALAD DRESSING

A flavorful basic dressing for tossed salads.

¾ cup vegetable oil
¼ cup cider vinegar

2 teaspoons Salad Seasoning Blend (see recipe, above)

In a jar place all ingredients. Shake well. Serve over mixed greens, cold cooked vegetables, sliced tomatoes, etc. Makes 1 cup.

SPANISH DRESSING (Vinaigrette Espagnole)

1 garlic clove, peeled
1 teaspoon diced canned pimiento
1 teaspoon dry mustard
1 teaspoon chili powder

Tarragon to taste
Pepper to taste
1 cup Basic French Dressing (see recipe, page 85)

Crush garlic and combine with remaining ingredients. Makes 1 cup.

MAIN DISHES: MEAT, SEAFOOD, POULTRY, MEATLESS

MEAT *CARROT STUFFED MEAT LOAF ·
HIGHLY RECOMMENDED BAKED STEW · HERBED
MEAT LOAF · MEDITERRANEAN BEEF STEW ·
SAVORY POT ROAST · LAMB STEAKS WITH
CURRY-APPLESAUCE · ORANGE-THYME LAMB
CHOPS · FRUITED PORK CHOPS · PORK CHOPS
IN WHITE WINE · VEAL WITH HERBS*

CARROT STUFFED MEAT LOAF

Extra A and B vitamins in this one.

1¼ cups (5 medium) peeled, chopped carrots	½ cup fresh orange juice
¾ cup wheat germ	2 eggs, beaten
½ cup chopped onion	1¼ pounds ground beef
1 teaspoon grated orange peel	¼ cup orange marmalade (optional)
¼ teaspoon crushed thyme leaves	

Parboil carrots in 1 inch boiling water for 5 minutes; drain and set aside to cool. Preheat oven to 350° F.

In a large bowl combine wheat germ, onion, orange peel, thyme, orange juice, and eggs. To the cooled carrots add ¼ cup of the wheat germ mixture; mix well and set aside. To the remaining wheat germ mixture add ground beef; mix well.

In an ungreased 8½" x 4½" x 2½" loaf pan spoon two-thirds of the meat mixture. Make a lengthwise well down the center. Spoon in carrot mixture; cover with remaining meat mixture; pat down firmly. Bake until meat is firm, about 1 hour and 15 minutes.

Heat broiler. Spread marmalade on top of meat loaf. Broil until marmalade is bubbling and glazed, about 5 minutes. Let stand in pan for 10 minutes before turning out onto a serving dish. Makes 6 portions.

HIGHLY RECOMMENDED BAKED STEW

The vegetables can be added 1 hour before serving time, if you prefer them less soft.

2 pounds stew meat, cut in chunks
3 medium potatoes, cut in chunks
3 carrots, cut in chunks
1 large onion, diced
1 cup rutabagas cut in chunks
3 tablespoons tapioca

2 cups low-sodium canned tomatoes or low-sodium tomato juice
½ cup water
1 teaspoon white or light brown sugar
Pepper to taste
2 teaspoons bourbon (optional)

In a large bowl combine ingredients. Bake in a covered pan 3½ to 5 hours at 250° F. Add bourbon 5 minutes before serving. Makes 4 to 6 portions.

HERBED MEAT LOAF

A flavorful, inexpensive dish.

2 tablespoons onion flakes, or ⅓ cup chopped onion
1½ cups plus 2 tablespoons water
1 pound ground beef
½ cup unsalted cooked rice
2 teaspoons crushed basil leaves

¼ teaspoon crushed thyme leaves
⅛ teaspoon ground black pepper
1 egg, lightly beaten

Preheat oven to 325° F. In a large bowl combine onion flakes and 2 tablespoons water; let stand for 10 minutes to soften. Add remaining ingredients and ½ cup water; mix well.

Shape into a loaf. Place in a greased baking pan. Bake until firm, about 50 minutes. Makes 4 portions.

MEDITERRANEAN BEEF STEW

A hearty meal in one dish.

2 tablespoons instant minced onion, or ⅓ cup chopped onion
½ teaspoon instant minced garlic, or 2 garlic cloves, minced
1½ cups plus 2 tablespoons water
3 tablespoons flour
¼ teaspoon ground black pepper
2 pounds lean stewing beef, cut into 1½-inch cubes
2 tablespoons vegetable oil
¾ cup dry red wine
1 bay leaf
1½ teaspoons crushed oregano leaves
¼ teaspoon crushed thyme leaves
6 large potatoes, peeled and cut into 1-inch chunks (6 cups)
6 medium carrots, peeled and cut into 1-inch chunks (3 cups)
1 tablespoon parsley flakes, or ½ cup chopped parsley

Combine minced onion and garlic with 2 tablespoons water; let stand for 10 minutes to soften; set aside.

Mix flour with black pepper. Coat beef with flour; set aside.

In a large heavy saucepan or Dutch oven heat oil until hot. Add beef; brown well on all sides; remove and set aside. Add onion and garlic; sauté 2 minutes. Add 1½ cups water, ½ cup of wine, bay leaf, 1 teaspoon of the oregano, and the thyme. Bring to the boiling point, stirring to scrape the drippings from the bottom of the pan. Return beef to pot. Bring to the boiling point. Reduce heat and simmer, covered, until beef is almost tender, about 1½ hours. Add potatoes and carrots. Return to the boiling point. Reduce heat and simmer, covered, until vegetables and beef are tender, about 30 minutes. Stir in parsley, remaining ¼ cup wine, and ½ teaspoon oregano. Cover and simmer for 5 minutes. Makes 8 portions.

SAVORY POT ROAST

Toss a salad and you have a meal.

2 tablespoons vegetable oil
3 pounds beef brisket
1 cup chopped onions
3 cups plus 2 tablespoons water
¼ teaspoon crushed rosemary leaves
6 large carrots, sliced (3 cups)
1 tablespoon flour

In a large saucepan heat oil until hot. Add meat; brown on all sides, about 8 minutes. Add onions; sauté until tender, about 5 minutes. Add 3 cups water and rosemary; bring to a boil. Reduce heat and simmer, covered, until meat is almost tender, about 2½ hours.

Skim off fat. Add carrots. Simmer, covered, until meat and vegetables are tender, about 20 minutes. Combine flour with 2 tablespoons water; add to saucepan and mix well. Cook and stir until thickened, about 2 minutes. Makes 9 portions.

LAMB STEAKS WITH CURRY-APPLESAUCE

A mildly seasoned curry.

3 tablespoons unsalted butter or margarine	3 tart apples, peeled and chopped
6 lamb steaks, cut ½–¾ inch thick	1¾ cups unsalted chicken broth
2 medium onions, chopped	2 tablespoons low-sodium tomato paste
1½ tablespoons curry powder	½ cup heavy cream
½ teaspoon ground ginger	

Melt butter or margarine in large skillet. Sauté lamb steaks until they are brown on both sides. Remove to platter.

Add chopped onions to skillet and cook until transparent. Add curry powder and ginger, stirring well. Add apples, broth, and tomato paste and bring to boil. Return lamb steaks and cover with sauce. Cover pan and simmer 25 minutes.

Uncover pan for 5 minutes and reduce sauce slightly. Add cream and season with additional curry powder. Serve with rice, unsalted peanuts, raisins, and coconut. Makes 6 portions.

ORANGE-THYME LAMB CHOPS

Serve with peas cooked with mint and dilled cucumbers.

6 shoulder lamb chops
(about 1½ pounds), cut
¾-inch thick
½ teaspoon shredded orange
peel
¼ cup orange juice
½ teaspoon crushed thyme
leaves

Pepper to taste
1 3-ounce can (about ½
cup) sliced mushrooms,
drained
Orange wedges for garnish

Trim excess fat from chops. Combine orange peel, juice, and thyme; pour over chops. Marinate for 1 hour at room temperature, or several hours in refrigerator, turning chops once or twice. Drain, reserving marinade.

Brown chops in small amount of fat; season with pepper. Add marinade and mushrooms. Cover; simmer about 40 minutes. Uncover and cook about 5 minutes more. Garnish with orange wedges. Makes 6 portions.

FRUITED PORK CHOPS

Serve with a green vegetable and mint ice for dessert.

1 8¾-ounce can sliced
peaches in heavy syrup
1 teaspoon vegetable oil
4 pork chops (1¼ pounds),
cut ½ inch thick
½ cup chopped onion

½ cup uncooked regular
white rice
1 cup water
½ cup seedless grapes, or
diced unpeeled apple

Drain peaches, reserving syrup; set aside. In a large skillet heat oil until hot. Add pork chops; brown on both sides. Remove pork chops. Add onion to oil remaining in skillet; sauté until tender, about 3 minutes. Stir in rice, water, and reserved peach syrup; place pork chops over mixture; bring to a boil. Reduce heat and simmer, covered, for 30 minutes, until pork chops and rice are tender. Add grapes or apple and reserved peaches; simmer, covered, until hot, about 3 minutes. Makes 4 portions.

PORK CHOPS IN WHITE WINE

Serve with noodles or rice.

1 teaspoon sage
1 teaspoon crushed
rosemary
1 teaspoon garlic powder
¼ teaspoon ground black
pepper
4 lean pork chops (1½
pounds), 1-inch thick,
trimmed
1 tablespoon unsalted
butter or margarine
1 tablespoon olive oil
¾ cup dry white wine
1 teaspoon scallion rings

In a small bowl combine sage, rosemary, garlic powder, and black pepper. Rub the spice mixture in both sides of each chop.

In a large skillet heat margarine with olive oil until hot. Add chops; brown well on both sides. Drain off drippings. Add ½ cup of the wine. Bring to a boil. Reduce heat and simmer, covered, until chops are tender, about 30 minutes, basting occasionally. Remove chops; keep warm. Add remaining ¼ cup wine. Boil briskly over high heat, stirring constantly, until syrupy, about 3 minutes. Remove from heat; stir in scallion rings and pour over pork chops. Makes 4 portions.

VEAL WITH HERBS

Tender and flavorful.

2 pounds veal, cut into 1½-inch cubes
Freshly ground pepper to taste
2 tablespoons unsalted butter
2 tablespoons vegetable or peanut oil
1½ cups thinly sliced mushrooms
1 cup finely chopped onion
1 teaspoon finely minced garlic
½ cup dry white wine
¼ cup flour
1½ cups low-sodium chicken broth
1 cup crushed tomatoes
1 sprig fresh rosemary, or ½ teaspoon dried rosemary
2 parsley sprigs
1 bay leaf
12 small white onions, or 2 medium onions, quartered
2 tablespoons scallion rings

Sprinkle the veal with pepper. Heat the butter and oil in a skillet and cook the meat, a few pieces at a time, until browned on all sides. As meat is browned, set it aside.

Add mushrooms, chopped onion, and garlic to the skillet and cook, stirring, until onion is wilted. Add the wine, stirring, and cook to evaporate. Return the meat to the skillet and sprinkle evenly with flour. Gradually add the broth, stirring to blend. Add the tomatoes, rosemary, parsley sprigs, and bay leaf, and cover. Cook over low heat about 1 hour. Add the white onions, cover, and continue cooking about 45 minutes longer or until meat and onions are tender. Serve sprinkled with chopped scallions. Serve with rice or mashed potatoes. Makes 4 to 6 portions.

SEAFOOD *BAKED FISH CONTINENTAL · COD WITH A TANG · EASY SPAGHETTI WITH FISH · MUSHROOM MEDLEY · MUSTARD FISH*

BAKED FISH CONTINENTAL

Use striped bass or white perch—both are sodium-free.

2 tablespoons instant minced onion, or ⅓ cup chopped onion
2 tablespoons water
½ teaspoon crushed basil leaves
½ teaspoon paprika
⅛ teaspoon garlic powder, or 1 garlic clove, minced
2 tablespoons vegetable oil
1½ tablespoons lemon juice
1 pound fish fillets
1 teaspoon parsley flakes or scallion rings

Preheat oven to 350° F. In a bowl combine minced onions and water; let stand for 10 minutes to soften. Stir in basil, paprika, garlic, oil, and lemon juice.

Place fish fillets in a greased 10″ x 6″ x 2″ baking pan. Pour herb mixture over top. Bake until fish flakes easily with a fork, about 15 minutes. Sprinkle with parsley flakes just before serving. Makes 4 portions.

COD WITH A TANG

Other fish can be substituted.

12 ounces fresh codfish
fillets or steaks
½ cup red wine vinegar or
fresh lemon juice
⅓ cup dry white wine

¼ teaspoon crushed
marjoram leaves
½ cup soft low-sodium
bread crumbs
Paprika

Place fish in a snug-fitting shallow baking pan in a single layer. In a small bowl combine vinegar, wine, and marjoram. Pour over fish; cover and set aside for 1 hour, turning fish after 30 minutes. Preheat oven to 350° F.

Drain off marinade, reserving 2½ tablespoons. In a small bowl combine bread crumbs and the reserved marinade. Spoon on the fish; sprinkle with paprika. Bake until fish is almost cooked, about 12 minutes. Heat broiler to hot. Place baking pan under broiler until fish flakes when tested with a fork and bread crumbs are browned, about 1 minute. Makes 4 portions.

EASY SPAGHETTI WITH FISH

Only 20 minutes preparation time needed.

2 tablespoons unsalted
butter or margarine
¾ cup chopped onions or
scallions
1 16-ounce package frozen
fish fillets, thawed and
drained, or 1 pound fresh
sole fillets
2 tablespoons fresh lemon
juice

Freshly ground pepper
½ cup shredded low-sodium
Cheddar cheese
1 large tomato, cut into
wedges
8 ounces spaghetti
3 quarts boiling water
2 tablespoons chopped
scallion tops

In a small saucepan, melt 1 tablespoon butter. Add onions; sauté over medium heat, stirring occasionally, until onions are tender, about 5 minutes. Preheat oven to 425° F.

Lightly sprinkle one side of each fillet with lemon juice and freshly ground pepper. Cut fillets in half lengthwise. Spread 2 teaspoons sautéed onions and about 1 tablespoon cheese on each fillet half. Reserve the remaining onions and cheese. Roll up fillets; fasten each with a toothpick. Place in a lightly buttered 9-inch pie plate; dot fillets with remaining butter. Bake, uncovered, for 15 minutes.

Remove from oven. Sprinkle the remaining cheese on top of fillets. Add tomato wedges and bake 5 more minutes, or until fish flakes easily when tested with a fork.

Meanwhile, gradually add spaghetti to rapidly boiling water so that water continues to boil. Cook, uncovered, stirring occasionally, until tender. Drain in colander. Toss cooked spaghetti with reserved onions. Serve spaghetti with fish and tomato wedges. Makes 4 portions.

MUSHROOM MEDLEY

Toss fresh mushroom slices in lemon juice to keep from discoloring.

½ cup vegetable oil
¼ cup cider vinegar
2 teaspoons celery seeds (optional)
¼ cup chopped onions
2 cloves garlic, minced
¼ teaspoon ground black pepper

½ pound fresh mushrooms, or 1 cup canned mushrooms
12 cherry tomatoes, halved
1 cup sliced zucchini
½ large red onion, sliced
2 7-ounce cans eel or herring, drained

In a 1-cup measure combine oil, vinegar, celery seeds, onions, garlic, and black pepper; stir to blend; set aside.

Rinse, pat dry, and slice mushrooms (makes about 2½ cups). In a large bowl combine mushrooms with tomatoes, zucchini, and onion. Add fish; toss gently.

Pour just enough dressing over the salad to coat completely. Refrigerate remaining dressing in a covered jar. Serve in a lettuce-lined bowl, if desired. Makes 4 portions (8 cups).

MUSTARD FISH

Good accompaniments are small boiled new potatoes, salad, and chilled cooked peas.

4 medium-size ripe tomatoes, peeled, seeded, and sliced ½ inch thick
⅛ teaspoon sugar
4 8-ounce fillets sea bass, well dried
Freshly ground white pepper
¾ cup dry white wine
6 tablespoons melted unsalted butter or margarine
1½ teaspoons Dijon-style mustard
1 teaspoon crushed sweet basil leaves
¼ teaspoon crushed thyme leaves
2 tablespoons fresh minced parsley or fresh basil sprigs

Preheat oven to 350° F. Sprinkle tomatoes with sugar; set aside. Sprinkle fillets generously with pepper.

In a greased shallow ovenproof skillet arrange fillets close together in single layer. Combine wine, butter, mustard, basil, and thyme; pour over fish. Bake uncovered 10 minutes.

Arrange tomatoes, slightly overlapping, over fish. Return fish to oven and bake just until flesh separates when tested with knife, about 8 minutes. Remove fillets and tomatoes to warm serving plates. Stir pan juices over high heat until slightly reduced and blended to thin sauce. Spoon over fish. Sprinkle with parsley and white pepper. Makes 4 portions.

POULTRY *CHICKEN MEDITERRANEAN · CURRIED CHICKEN · LEMON CHICKEN · MARINATED CHICKEN SALAD · STIR-FRIED CHICKEN AND VEGETABLES · SWANK CHICKEN CHILI · TANDOORI CHICKEN*

CHICKEN MEDITERRANEAN

Low-sodium tomatoes and mushrooms are added to a basic chicken sauté.

3 teaspoons No Salt Herb Blend (see recipe below)	¾ cup water
3 pounds chicken parts	1 teaspoon paprika
2 tablespoons vegetable oil	Fresh ground black pepper
2½ cups diced low-sodium canned tomatoes, or 4 fresh tomatoes, diced	1 cup diced green pepper
	1 cup sliced mushrooms
	1 teaspoon cornstarch
	Parsley flakes

Rub 1 teaspoon of the Herb Blend into all sides of the chicken. In a large skillet heat oil until hot. Add chicken and brown on all sides. Drain off drippings. Add tomatoes, ½ cup water, paprika, black pepper, and remaining 2 teaspoons Herb Blend. Bring to a boil. Reduce heat and simmer, covered, until chicken is tender, about 35 minutes.

Add green pepper; simmer, covered, for 5 minutes. Add mushrooms; simmer, covered, 5 minutes longer.

Combine cornstarch with ¼ cup water. Add to skillet. Cook and stir until thickened, 2 to 3 minutes. Sprinkle with parsley flakes and serve with steamed rice, if desired. Makes 4 portions.

No Salt Herb Blend:

Use in French and Italian dishes; sprinkle on meats, eggs, fish, or cottage cheese.

4 tablespoons oregano	4 teaspoons garlic powder
4 tablespoons onion powder	2 teaspoons thyme
4 teaspoons marjoram	2 teaspoons rosemary
4 teaspoons basil	1 teaspoon sage
4 teaspoons ground savory	1 teaspoon ground pepper

In a medium bowl combine all ingredients. Crush a small amount at a time in a mortar with a pestle or with the back of a spoon. Spoon into a shaker or tightly covered container. Makes about 1 cup.

CURRIED CHICKEN

Serve garnished with toasted coconut and chopped unsalted peanuts.

¼ cup flour	Pinch cayenne pepper
1½ teaspoons curry powder	1 2½-pound chicken, cut
1½ teaspoons onion powder,	into serving pieces
or ¼ cup chopped onion	¼ cup vegetable oil
½ teaspoon ground turmeric	¾ cup hot water
¼ teaspoon ground ginger	¼ cup dry white wine
¼ teaspoon powdered mustard	

Combine flour and seasonings. Coat chicken well with seasoned flour. Shake off excess; reserve remaining flour mixture.

In a large skillet heat oil. Add chicken; brown well on all sides. Remove from heat; push chicken to one side of skillet. Gradually stir in reserved flour; blend well. Stir in water and wine. Return skillet to heat; bring to the boiling point. Reduce heat and simmer, covered, until chicken is tender, about 35 minutes. Makes 4 portions.

LEMON CHICKEN

Bitters "marry" and heighten flavors.

1 broiler fryer, quartered
2 lemons
⅓ cup flour
½ teaspoon paprika
¼ cup vegetable oil

2 tablespoons brown sugar
¾ cup water
1½ teaspoons angostura
   bitters

Preheat oven to 375° F. Wash chicken and dry well. Cut one lemon in half and squeeze juice from one half over each chicken piece. Combine flour and paprika in paper bag and add chicken pieces one at a time. Shake well to coat with flour.

Heat oil in skillet and brown chicken parts. Arrange pieces in baking dish or Dutch oven. Thinly slice remaining lemon and place in layer over chicken. Dissolve brown sugar in water and add bitters. Pour over chicken. Cover and bake or simmer over very low heat until chicken is tender, about 45 minutes. Serve hot with juice. Makes 4 portions.

MARINATED CHICKEN SALAD

Make ahead—the flavor gets better and better.

¾ cup vegetable oil
¼ cup cider vinegar
4 teaspoons onion powder,
   or ¼ cup chopped onion
1½ teaspoons crushed basil
   leaves
1½ teaspoons crushed
   oregano leaves

¾ teaspoon garlic powder, or
   3 garlic cloves, minced
Fresh ground black pepper
2 cups cooked diced
   chicken
½ pound mushrooms, sliced
2 medium tomatoes, cut
   into ½-inch cubes

Combine oil, vinegar, onion, basil, oregano, garlic, and black pepper. Toss chicken, mushrooms, and tomatoes with seasoned oil mixture. Cover and refrigerate at least 1 hour before serving. Makes 4 portions.

STIR-FRIED CHICKEN AND VEGETABLES

No soy sauce but lots of flavor.

2 tablespoons vegetable oil
1 cup coarsely chopped
  onion
1 teaspoon minced garlic
1 pound boneless and
  skinless chicken breasts,
  cut into ¾-inch pieces

½ cup cold water
1 teaspoon cornstarch
¾ teaspoon ground ginger
1 teaspoon angostura bitters
2 medium tomatoes, cut
  into wedges
1 cup diced green pepper

Heat oil in a large skillet. Add onions and garlic; sauté until barely tender. Remove to a bowl, leaving as much oil as possible in skillet. Scatter chicken pieces in skillet; do not stir for 1 minute. Then stir and cook until chicken is almost cooked through, about 2 minutes. Remove skillet from heat.

In a measuring cup combine water, cornstarch, ginger, and bitters; mix well and set aside. Return onion and garlic to skillet; add tomatoes and green pepper. Stir in ginger mixture. Cook and stir, uncovered, until sauce is thickened and green pepper is barely tender; about 2 minutes. Makes 4 portions.

SWANK CHICKEN CHILI

This chili-flavored chicken may be served over either red beans, rice, or both.

¼ cup vegetable oil
9 chicken or 3 turkey
  thighs, skinned, boned,
  and cut into 1-inch pieces
2 large onions, chopped
3 small green peppers,
  seeded and chopped
2 garlic cloves, minced
1 teaspoon lemon juice
1 tablespoon chili powder

1½ teaspoons ground cumin
  seed
1½ teaspoons crushed
  oregano
  Fresh ground black pepper
1 28-ounce can salt-free
  tomatoes
¼ cup shredded low-sodium
  cheese

Heat oil in skillet and brown chicken. Add onions, peppers, garlic, lemon juice, and seasonings; stir well and add tomatoes. Cover and simmer 45 minutes or until chicken is tender. Uncover and simmer until mixture thickens. Serve sprinkled with cheese. Makes 6 portions.

TANDOORI CHICKEN

In India, this would be prepared in a clay Tandoori oven. Here we use a charcoal grill or a broiler.

1 tablespoon instant minced onion, or ¼ cup chopped onion
½ teaspoon instant minced garlic, or 2 garlic cloves, chopped
3½ teaspoons water
3 tablespoons vegetable oil
3 or more tablespoons curry powder
1 cup plain yogurt
1 tablespoon lemon juice
3 pounds chicken parts, skinned
½ cup melted unsalted butter

In a small bowl or cup combine onion, garlic, and water; let stand for 10 minutes to soften.

In a small skillet heat oil until hot; add curry powder; sauté until curry powder turns slightly darker, about 30 seconds.

In the container of an electric blender add the onion and garlic, the curry powder mixture, ¼ cup of the yogurt, and lemon juice. Blend until well combined, about 1 minute; stir in remaining ¾ cup yogurt.

Pierce chicken all over with fork tines. Arrange in a pan; cover with yogurt mixture. Cover and refrigerate for about 1½ hours. Pierce chicken with fork tines again; turn pieces over. Let marinate for an additional 1½ hours.

Preheat broiler or barbecue grill. Brush chicken with some of the melted butter. Place chicken pieces on broiler rack in a pan or on a barbecue grill, 4 to 6 inches from heat. Grill, brushing every 5 minutes with yogurt marinade and melted butter, until one side of the chicken is browned, about 15 minutes. Turn pieces over. Broil, brushing with marinade and butter until chicken is browned and cooked through, about 15 minutes longer.

Serve with Naan (page 116), Spicy Rice and Peas (page 112), Cucumber Raita (page 84), and fresh fruit, if desired. Makes 4 to 6 portions.

MEATLESS *CHEESE STUFFED GREEN PEPPERS • CREAMED EGGS AND MUSHROOMS • MEATLESS MEXICAN FILLING • PASTA PRIMAVERA • POTATO-APPLE CASSEROLE • BASIC CREPES • BLENDER HOLLANDAISE SAUCE • VEGETABLE CREPES*

CHEESE STUFFED GREEN PEPPERS

A hearty entree for a meatless meal.

6 large green bell peppers	1 teaspoon paprika
3 cups cooked brown rice or bulgur wheat	½ teaspoon oregano
	Dash Tabasco sauce
2 cups shredded low-sodium cheese (8 ounces)	3 eggs, slightly beaten
	¾ cup water
1¼ cups finely chopped low-sodium canned tomatoes	Chopped parsley (optional)

Preheat oven to 375° F. Cut a thin slice off the top of each pepper; remove seeds. Precook peppers in boiling water for 10 minutes. Drain and rinse with cold water; set aside. Combine rice, cheese, ¾ cup tomatoes, oregano, paprika, Tabasco sauce, and eggs. Spoon into peppers; place in a snug-fitting casserole.

Combine water with remaining ½ cup tomatoes and pour over peppers. Bake, uncovered, until cheese is melted and rice mixture is heated through, about 45 minutes. Garnish with chopped parsley, if desired. Makes 6 portions.

CREAMED EGGS AND MUSHROOMS

Serve in patty shells, if sodium restriction is not severe, or on baked potatoes, bulgur wheat, or no-sodium bread, toasted.

½ pound fresh mushrooms	¼ teaspoon rosemary
4 tablespoons unsalted butter or margarine	5 hard-cooked eggs
	Parsley or paprika for garnish
3 tablespoons flour	
1½ cups cream	
Dash Tabasco sauce	

Rinse mushrooms and pat dry; cut in half or slice. Heat butter, add mushrooms, and sauté until mushrooms are golden, about 5 minutes; set aside.

In a medium saucepan heat remaining 4 tablespoons butter. Stir in flour until smooth. Blend in cream; cook and stir constantly, until thickened. Stir in Tabasco sauce and rosemary; simmer 1 minute.

Cut eggs into wedges; stir eggs and reserved mushrooms into sauce. Serve hot garnished with parsley or paprika. Makes 6 portions.

MEATLESS MEXICAN FILLING

Use for tacos, tostados, or burritos.

2 tablespoons vegetable oil
1 large onion, chopped
2 large carrots, thinly sliced
1 clove garlic, minced or pressed
2½ teaspoons chili powder
½ teaspoon angostura bitters
¾ teaspoon cumin
¾ teaspoon crushed oregano leaves

4 medium zucchini (1½ pounds), cut into ½-inch cubes
1 large green or red pepper, seeded and chopped
1 8-ounce can unsalted whole kernel corn
1 16-ounce can unsalted kidney beans, drained

Heat oil and add onion, carrots, garlic, chili powder, bitters, cumin, and oregano. Cook, stirring, until onion is limp. Add remaining ingredients and cook until zucchini is tender-crisp, 7 to 8 minutes. Serve hot with shredded lettuce and chopped tomatoes. Makes filling for 10 to 12 tacos, tostados, or burritos.

PASTA PRIMAVERA

Primavera = Springtime.

1 pound (about 4 cups) fresh broccoli, cut into small florets
1 pound (about 3 cups) fresh green beans, cut into 1-inch pieces
2 red peppers (about 2 cups), cut into 2-inch strips
Water

8 tablespoons unsalted butter or margarine
1 cup chopped onions
½ teaspoon minced garlic
¾ pound (about 4 cups) fresh mushrooms, sliced
½ pound uncooked enriched linguine or fettuccine

Parboil broccoli, green beans, and red peppers in 1 inch boiling water, covered, until crisp-tender, about 5 minutes. Drain and keep warm.

In a large skillet melt butter. Add onions and garlic; sauté until tender, about 3 minutes. Add mushrooms; sauté until tender, about 5 minutes.

Meanwhile, in a large saucepan cook linguine according to package directions in unsalted boiling water. Drain and place in a large serving bowl. Add reserved vegetables; toss to mix. Makes 6 portions.

POTATO-APPLE CASSEROLE

Quick, easy, and excellent.

4 tablespoons unsalted butter or margarine
2 cups hot mashed potatoes
2 cups unsweetened applesauce

2 tablespoons sugar
½ teaspoon nutmeg

Preheat oven to 400° F. Whip butter into mashed potatoes and then add remaining ingredients. Turn into a buttered casserole and bake until nicely browned, about 15 minutes. Makes 4 to 6 portions.

BASIC CREPES

Make several batches at a time and freeze.

2 eggs
½ cup all-purpose flour
¼ cup reconstituted low-sodium milk powder
¼ cup water

1 tablespoon melted unsalted butter or margarine
1 teaspoon sugar

Measure all ingredients into mixer bowl; beat until smooth. Batter will be thin. Refrigerate 2 hours, if possible.

Pour scant ¼ cup batter into well-warmed, lightly greased 8-inch crepe pan or skillet. Tilt pan to coat bottom evenly with batter. Cook over medium heat until brown; turn crepe to brown second side. Cool pan slightly between crepes. Spoon any filling onto center of crepe and roll. Makes 8 or 9 crepes.

NOTE: To freeze: Layer crepes with waxed paper and store in a tightly closed plastic bag or in aluminum foil. Date, label, and freeze. To heat, place unsalted wrapped crepes on baking sheet. Bake in 325° F. oven until hot, 12 to 15 minutes.

BLENDER HOLLANDAISE SAUCE

Orange juice makes a version of Maltaise sauce.

3 egg yolks
1-2 tablespoons lemon or orange juice
Dash cayenne pepper
Dash angostura bitters

½ cup unsalted butter or margarine
Few drops dry vermouth (optional)

Place egg yolks, lemon juice, cayenne, and bitters in blender container. Cover; quickly turn blender on and off. Heat butter until melted and almost boiling. Turn blender on high speed; slowly pour in butter, blending until thick and fluffy, about 30 seconds. Blend in vermouth. Makes 1 cup.

*When using orange juice you may wish to add a small amount of an orange-flavor liqueur.

VEGETABLE CREPES

Especially nice served with Blender Hollandaise Sauce (see recipe, page 107).

2 cups shredded cabbage
1 cup thinly sliced carrots
½ green pepper, thinly sliced
¼ cup chopped onion
¼ cup sliced mushrooms
¼ cup unsalted butter or margarine

1 tablespoon sugar
1 tablespoon lemon juice
½ teaspoon dill weed
⅛ teaspoon pepper
8 warm Basic Crepes (see recipe, page 107)

Sauté cabbage, carrots, green pepper, onion, and mushrooms in butter with sugar, covered, for about 5 minutes, until crisp-tender. Stir in lemon juice, dill weed, and pepper. Spoon mixture onto center of crepes; roll. Makes 8 portions.

# VEGETABLE SIDE DISHES

APRICOT STUFFED ZUCCHINI · CARROTS WITH ORANGE SAUCE · CLAM AND WALNUT STUFFED MUSHROOMS · FROZEN CUCUMBERS · MUSHROOMS À LA GRECQUE · SAUTÉED CUCUMBER RINGS · SPICY RICE AND PEAS · VEGETABLES ORIENTAL

APRICOT STUFFED ZUCCHINI

Serve with grilled meat.

4 large zucchini (1½ pounds)
1 cup water
½ cup chopped dried apricots

2 cups soft low-sodium bread crumbs
1 egg, beaten
2 tablespoons chopped walnuts

Preheat oven to 375° F. Trim off ends of zucchini; halve lengthwise. Carefully scoop out centers leaving a ¼-inch-thick shell; set shells aside. Chop pulp (makes about 1 cup); set aside.

In a small saucepan bring 1 cup water to a boil; add apricots. Simmer, covered, until almost tender, about 5 minutes. Add reserved zucchini pulp; simmer until zucchini and apricots are tender, about 2 minutes. Drain and set aside.

In a skillet cook zucchini shells in boiling water until almost tender, 2 to 3 minutes. Rinse shells with cold water; drain well. Place shells, hollowed sides up, in a baking pan. To reserved apricot mixture add bread crumbs, egg, and walnuts; mix well. Spoon into zucchini shells. Bake, uncovered, until zucchini is tender, about 15 minutes. Makes 4 portions.

CARROTS WITH ORANGE SAUCE

A good flavor combination.

2 tablespoons unsalted butter or margarine	2 tablespoons firmly packed light brown sugar
2 tablespoons flour	¼ teaspoon ground allspice
1 cup orange juice	3 cups cooked sliced carrots
1½ teaspoons angostura bitters	

Melt butter and stir in flour; gradually stir in orange juice, bitters, brown sugar, and allspice. Cook over low heat, stirring constantly, until sauce bubbles and thickens. Fold in carrots and simmer 15 minutes. Makes 6 portions.

CLAM AND WALNUT STUFFED MUSHROOMS

Hors d'oeuvre or entree, they're delicious.

1 pound medium mushrooms (about 20)	1 cup unsalted matzoh crumbs
8 tablespoons unsalted butter or margarine	½ cup chopped walnuts
1 garlic clove, minced	¼ cup chopped parsley
1 10-ounce can minced or whole baby clams, drained	¼ teaspoon ground black Pepper
	Lemon juice

Preheat oven to 350° F. Rinse, pat dry, and remove stems from mushrooms; chop stems (makes about 1 cup); set aside.

In a large skillet melt butter or margarine. Use about 3 tablespoons to brush mushroom caps; place on a shallow pan; set aside. In skillet, add garlic and reserved chopped mushroom stems to remaining butter. Sauté for 2 minutes. Stir in clams, matzoh crumbs, walnuts, parsley, and black pepper. Stuff into mushroom caps, piling high. Sprinkle with lemon juice. Bake until hot, about 12 minutes. If desired, garnish with walnut halves and parsley sprigs. Makes 20 hors d'oeuvres or 4 entree portions.

FROZEN CUCUMBERS

Pickles you don't process.

2 quarts sliced cucumbers (unpeeled)	2 teaspoons dill weed
Sliced onion (optional)	½ cup cider vinegar
	1½ cups granulated sugar

Combine cucumbers, onion, and dill weed; let stand 2 hours. Drain well. Warm vinegar and sugar to dissolve the sugar; pour over cucumbers packed in freezer containers, cover and freeze. Makes about 2 pints.

MUSHROOMS À LA GRECQUE

For an hors d'oeuvre, thread mushrooms, carrot chunks, and cherry tomatoes on skewers or spoon into a bowl.

1 pound fresh mushrooms, or 2 6- to 8-ounce cans whole mushrooms	1 large garlic clove, minced
⅓ cup olive oil	1 teaspoon sugar
⅓ cup dry white wine	½ teaspoon coriander seed (optional)
¼ cup water	Fresh ground black pepper
1½ tablespoons lemon juice	2 cups sliced carrots
¾ cup chopped onion	20 cherry tomatoes

Rinse, pat dry, and halve fresh mushrooms or drain canned mushrooms; set aside. In a large saucepan combine oil, wine, water, lemon juice, onion, garlic, sugar, coriander seeds, and black pepper. Bring to boiling point; add carrots. Cover and simmer for 15 minutes.

Add mushrooms and cherry tomatoes. Return to boiling point; reduce heat. Cover and simmer for 5 minutes. Chill thoroughly at least overnight. Makes about 1 quart—8 to 10 hors d'oeuvre portions.

SAUTÉED CUCUMBER RINGS

Cucumbers are as delicious hot as cold.

2 firm, unblemished cucumbers (about 1¼ pounds)	2 tablespoons light brown sugar
3 tablespoons unsalted butter	Freshly ground pepper
	2 tablespoons red wine vinegar

Trim off the ends of the cucumbers. If the cucumbers are young and tender, do not peel. If the skins are tough, however, peel them. Halve the cucumbers crosswise.

Using a small melon ball cutter, knife, or spoon, cut or scrape away and discard the soft core with seeds. Cut the cucumbers into ¾-inch-thick slices. Heat the butter in a skillet and add the cucumber rings. Cook, shaking and tossing the skillet, about 30 seconds. Sprinkle with half the sugar and pepper. Cook, stirring and tossing about 30 seconds, and add the remaining sugar and the vinegar. Cook, tossing and stirring about 1 minute, no longer. Do not overcook. Serve hot. Makes about 8 portions.

SPICY RICE AND PEAS

Serve with Tandoori Chicken (page 103) or any meat dish.

3 tablespoons vegetable oil	2 tablespoons unsalted butter or margarine
2 cups raw long-grain rice	1 tablespoon lemon or lime juice
1 teaspoon turmeric	
1 teaspoon chili powder	
4 cups boiling water	
1 10-ounce package frozen peas	

In a large saucepan heat oil. Add rice, turmeric, and chili powder. Sauté until spices coat rice and rice is lightly toasted, about 3 minutes. Add 3 cups of the water. Bring rice to a boil. Simmer, covered, for 15 minutes. Run frozen peas under warm water until separated. Add to cooked rice, along with remaining 1 cup water. Simmer, covered, until peas are hot, about 5 minutes. Add butter or margarine and lemon or lime juice; stir until melted. Makes 6 portions.

VEGETABLES ORIENTAL

Crisp and flavorful.

2 tablespoons onion flakes, or ⅓ cup chopped onion
½ teaspoon instant minced garlic, or 2 garlic cloves, minced
1½ cups plus 2 tablespoons water
1 pound broccoli

3 tablespoons vegetable oil
1 cup thinly sliced carrots
2 cups coarsely shredded cabbage
2 tablespoons cornstarch
2 teaspoons sugar
1½ teaspoons ground ginger
Fresh ground black pepper

Combine onion flakes and minced garlic with 2 tablespoons water; let stand for 10 minutes to soften. Meanwhile, cut broccoli in flowerets; trim stems; cut crosswise into thin slices (makes 6 cups); set aside.

In a large skillet or wok heat oil until hot. Add onion and garlic; sauté for 3 minutes. Add carrots and reserved broccoli; cook and stir for 10 minutes. Add cabbage; cook and stir for 2 minutes.

In a bowl, mix cornstarch with sugar, ginger, and black pepper; blend in 1½ cups cold water. Stir into skillet. Cook and stir until mixture boils and thickens. Makes 6 portions.

 # BREADS AND DESSERTS

BREADS *BRAN BREAD · HERBED BREAD · NAAN · ONION AND POPPY SEED BREAD · SPICED CRANBERRY-NUT BREAD*

BRAN BREAD

A nutty flavor, interesting texture, and toasty color.

4¼–5½ cups unsifted all-purpose flour
2 tablespoons sugar
1 teaspoon grated lemon rind
2 packages active dry yeast
2 cups whole bran cereal
1 cup reconstituted low-sodium milk
½ cup water
2 tablespoons honey
⅓ cup unsalted butter or margarine
2 eggs (at room temperature)

In a large bowl combine 1 cup flour, sugar, lemon rind, and yeast; add cereal. Combine milk, water, honey, and butter or margarine in a saucepan and heat over low flame until very warm (120°–130° F.). Butter or margarine does not need to melt. Gradually add to dry ingredients and beat 2 minutes at medium speed of electric mixer, scraping bowl occasionally. Add eggs and enough additional flour to make a thick batter. Beat at high speed 2 minutes, scraping bowl occasionally.

Stir in enough additional flour to make a soft dough. Turn out onto lightly floured board; knead until smooth and elastic, about 8 to 10 minutes. Place in greased bowl, turning to grease dough all over. Cover; let rise in warm place until doubled in bulk, about 45 minutes. Punch dough down; turn onto floured board. Divide in half and shape into loaves. Place in greased loaf pans. Cover; let rise in warm place until doubled, about 1 hour.

Preheat oven to 375° F. Bake on the lowest rack position 30 to 35 minutes, or until done. Remove from pans, brush tops with melted butter, and cool on racks. Makes 2 loaves.

HERBED BREAD

Wonderful for sandwiches.

1 medium potato, peeled	2 tablespoons parsley flakes
1 cup boiling water	2 teaspoons onion powder
4½–5 cups unsifted all-purpose flour	½ teaspoon crushed marjoram leaves
1 package active dry yeast	½ teaspoon crushed rosemary leaves
2 tablespoons sugar	⅛ teaspoon ground black pepper
1 cup reconstituted low-sodium milk	1 egg, lightly beaten
6 tablespoons unsalted butter or margarine	2 tablespoons sesame seeds

Cook potato in boiling water. Drain, reserving ½ cup liquid. Mash potato to make ½ cup; reserve.

In the large bowl of an electric mixer combine 2 cups of the flour with yeast and sugar.

In a medium saucepan combine milk, reserved ½ cup potato water, and 2 tablespoons of the butter or margarine. Heat over low flame until lukewarm (butter or margarine does not need to melt). Pour into bowl containing flour mixture.

With electric mixer set at low speed, beat until blended. Beat at high speed for 3 minutes. With a wooden spoon stir in reserved mashed potato and enough flour, about 2 cups, to make a soft dough. Turn out onto a lightly floured board; knead in enough flour, about ½ cup, so that dough becomes smooth and elastic, about 5 minutes. Place in a lightly greased bowl, turning to grease dough all over. Cover lightly with a towel; let rise in a warm place until double in bulk.

Meanwhile, in a small saucepan melt remaining 4 tablespoons butter. Stir in parsley flakes, onion powder, marjoram, rosemary, and black pepper; reserve for later use.

Punch dough down; divide into two equal parts. On a lightly floured board roll each half into a 12" x 8" rectangle. Spread each rectangle with herbed butter mixture. Roll up, jelly-roll fashion, from narrow end. Place each roll, seam-side down, in a greased 8½" x 4½" x 2½" loaf pan. Cover lightly with a towel; let rise until double in bulk, about 1 hour.

Preheat oven to 400° F. Brush dough with egg; sprinkle with sesame seeds. Bake until golden, about 30 minutes. Remove breads from pans; cool on wire racks. Makes 2 loaves.

NAAN

In India this would be baked in a clay oven, but you can do it under your broiler.

3 cups all-purpose flour	1 egg, beaten
1 tablespoon sugar	½ cup warm milk
2 teaspoons active dry yeast	¼ cup plain yogurt
1½ teaspoons no-sodium Baking Powder (see recipe, page 49)	2 tablespoons vegetable oil Water
	1½ teaspoons poppy seeds

In a large bowl combine flour, sugar, yeast, and baking powder. Add egg, ¼ cup of the warm milk, yogurt, and oil. Combine and form into a ball. Turn out onto a floured board. Knead, adding 1 tablespoon of remaining milk at a time, until dough is soft and elastic, but not sticky, about 5 minutes. Form into a ball; brush with oil. Place in a large greased bowl, turning to grease dough all over. Cover with a damp cloth. Place in a warm, draft-free area until dough is about 1½ times its original size, about 3 hours.

Divide dough into 6 equal portions. On a floured board roll each portion out into an elongated shape, about 12 inches long by 4 inches wide by ¼ inch thick. Trim edges with a knife to form a teardrop shape. Place on an oiled foil-lined baking sheet. Cover with a damp cloth; let rise for 15 minutes.

Preheat broiler to hot. Brush the top of each bread with water; sprinkle on ¼ teaspoon poppy seeds. Place under the broiler, about 4 inches from heat, until lightly browned, about 2½ minutes on each side. Serve hot with Tandoori Chicken (see recipe, page 103). Makes 6 breads.

ONION AND POPPY SEED BREAD

Also an excellent bread for sandwiches.

¼ cup poppy seeds	6½ cups unsifted all-purpose flour
3 cups or more water	
¼ cup instant minced onion, or ½ cup finely minced onion	2 cups whole wheat or graham flour, or unsifted light rye flour
1 teaspoon instant minced garlic, or 2 garlic cloves, minced	¼ cup granulated sugar
	2 eggs
2 packages active dry yeast	3 tablespoons shortening

In a bowl combine poppy seeds with 1 cup water; let stand 45 minutes to soften; drain and set poppy seeds aside. In separate bowl combine onion and garlic with an equal amount of water; let stand 10 minutes to soften.

In the large bowl of an electric mixer dissolve yeast in 2 cups warm water (105°–115° F.), set aside for 5 minutes. Add 3 cups of the all-purpose flour, whole-wheat flour, sugar, 1 egg, reserved poppy seeds, onion, and garlic; beat until smooth, about 2 minutes. Add shortening; beat until smooth, about 2 minutes. With a wooden spoon stir in enough of the all-purpose flour to make a soft dough (about 3 cups). Turn the dough onto a floured board; knead in remaining flour, until smooth and elastic, about 10 minutes. Place dough in a lightly greased bowl, turning to grease dough all over. Cover lightly and let rise in a warm place until doubled in bulk, about 1 hour.

Punch down dough and turn out onto a lightly floured board. Divide dough into 3 equal pieces; cover and set aside for 10 minutes. With a floured rolling pin, roll out each piece into a 12" x 8" rectangle. Starting from narrow end, roll up dough, jelly-roll fashion. Place seam side down on lightly greased baking sheets. Tuck ends under and shape rolls gently upward with hands to add height. Cover and let rise in a warm place until doubled in bulk, about 45 minutes.

Preheat oven to 350° F. With a sharp knife, slash top of each bread on the diagonal four times. Lightly beat remaining egg with a teaspoon water. Brush evenly over each loaf. Bake until browned and bread sounds hollow when tapped with fingers, about 30 minutes. Cool on wire racks. Makes 3 loaves.

SPICED CRANBERRY-NUT BREAD

Excellent with coffee or a spiced punch, or serve with a scoop of orange ice for dessert.

1½ cups chopped cranberries
1½ cups granulated sugar
3 cups unsifted all-purpose flour
3¼ teaspoons no-sodium Baking Powder (see recipe, page 49)
2¼ teaspoons ground cinnamon
2 teaspoons grated orange peel
¾ teaspoon no-sodium baking soda (potassium bicarbonate)
¼ teaspoon ground cloves
⅓ cup shortening
1 cup orange juice
2 eggs, beaten
1½ cups chopped walnuts

Preheat oven to 350° F. Grease a 9" x 5" x 2¾" loaf pan; set aside. Combine cranberries with ¼ cup of the sugar; set aside.

In a large bowl combine flour, baking powder, cinnamon, orange peel, baking soda, cloves, and remaining 1¼ cups of the sugar. Cut in shortening with a pastry blender until mixture resembles cornmeal. Add orange juice and eggs; mix well. Stir reserved cranberries into batter along with walnuts.

Pour into prepared pan. Bake until done, about 1 hour and 10 minutes. Turn out of pan; cool on wire rack. Makes 1 loaf.

DESERTS FRESH TOMATO CAKE · SPICED CHOCOLATE ZUCCHINI CAKE · LACE DOUGHNUTS · RHUBARB MERINGUE SQUARES · BASIC PIE PASTRY · APPLE MACAROON PIE · DOROTHY'S PEACH PIE · NATURAL APPLE PIE · SQUASH PEANUT PIE · BANANA CREPES · CHOCOLATE MOUSSE · CREAM PUFFS · POACHED SPICED PEACHES · CRUNCHY CEREAL

FRESH TOMATO CAKE

Stays moist and fresh a long while.

7 medium-size ripe tomatoes (about 3½ pounds)	½ cup softened unsalted butter or margarine
Water	1 cup firmly packed light brown sugar
3 cups unsifted all-purpose flour	1 teaspoon ground allspice
3 teaspoons no-sodium Baking Powder (see recipe, page 49)	¾ teaspoon grated orange rind
1 teaspoon no-sodium baking soda (potassium bicarbonate)	½ teaspoon ground ginger
	2 eggs
	½ cup raisins
	½ cup chopped dates
	Confectioners' sugar

Preheat oven to 350° F. Place tomatoes in boiling water until skin loosens slightly, about 1 minute. Rinse with cold water and remove skins. Cut tomatoes into quarters; remove seeds and chop (makes about 3 cups); drain very well in a sieve or colander; set aside.

Mix flour, baking powder, and baking soda; set aside.

In a large mixing bowl cream butter, sugar, allspice, orange rind, and ginger until light and fluffy. Add eggs; mix well. Stir in raisins, dates, and reserved tomatoes; mix well (mixture will look curdled).

Gradually add reserved dry ingredients; mix until completely blended. Pour into a greased 9" x 5" x 3" loaf pan. Bake until done, about 1 hour 10 minutes. Let stand for 5 minutes. Turn onto a wire rack to cool. Sprinkle with confectioners' sugar before serving. Makes one 9-inch loaf cake—8 to 10 portions.

SPICED CHOCOLATE ZUCCHINI CAKE

A moist cake with a jam filling.

2½ cups unsifted all-purpose
flour
½ cup unsweetened cocoa
3¾ teaspoons no-sodium
Baking Powder (see
recipe, page 49)
1½ teaspoons no-sodium
baking soda (potassium
bicarbonate)
¾ cup softened unsalted
butter or margarine
2 cups granulated sugar

2 teaspoons ground
cinnamon
¾ teaspoon ground nutmeg
3 eggs
2 cups (about ½ pound)
grated unpeeled zucchini
2 teaspoons pure vanilla
extract
½ cup reconstituted no-
sodium milk
Strawberry jam
Confectioners' sugar

Preheat oven to 350° F. Grease and lightly flour two 9-inch round cake pans; set aside. Mix flour, cocoa, baking powder, and baking soda; set aside.

In a large bowl cream butter, sugar, cinnamon, and nutmeg until light and fluffy. Add eggs; mix well. Stir in zucchini and vanilla extract. Alternately add dry ingredients with milk, beginning and ending with flour, using one-third of the dry ingredients and one half of the milk at a time. After each addition, beat until well blended.

Pour into prepared pans. Bake until a cake tester inserted into the center comes out clean, about 30 minutes. Let stand for 5 minutes. Turn onto wire racks to cool. Spread 1 layer with strawberry jam. Top with second layer. Sprinkle with confectioners' sugar. Makes one 9-inch round cake—8 to 10 portions.

LACE DOUGHNUTS

Crisp, thin, and pretty, these fried cookies are fun to serve.

2 eggs, well beaten
1 tablespoon granulated
sugar
1 cup reconstituted low-
sodium dry milk
2–2½ cups all-purpose flour

2 tablespoons no-sodium
Baking Powder (see
recipe, page 49)
2 cups cooking oil for deep-
frying
Confectioners' sugar

Combine in a bowl eggs, sugar, milk, and flour sifted with baking powder.

In a skillet or deep-fryer heat oil; pour the dough into a funnel with your finger over the hole. Then start the flow of the dough in the middle of the skillet. Go around and around with the stream of dough until you have a cookie about the size of a pancake. Cook until golden; turn over gently and brown the second side. Cool on a cloth or paper towel. Sprinkle with sugar or frost with confectioners' sugar icing made by combining confectioners' sugar and water or fruit juice. Makes about 3 dozen doughnuts.

RHUBARB MERINGUE SQUARES

Easier than rhubarb pie and they go further.

CRUST:

1 cup sifted all-purpose
flour
2 tablespoons granulated
sugar

½ cup (1 stick) unsalted
butter or margarine

FILLING:

3 egg yolks
1¾ cups granulated sugar
4½ tablespoons flour
1 teaspoon grated orange
peel

¾ cup reconstituted low-
sodium dry milk
4 cups fresh diced rhubarb

MERINGUE:

3 egg whites
¼ cup granulated sugar

¼ teaspoon vanilla

To prepare crust: Preheat oven to 325° F. Combine flour and sugar; cut in butter or margarine until mixture is crumbly. Press into an 11" x 7" baking pan. Bake 20 minutes.

To prepare filling meanwhile, beat egg yolks well. Slowly beat in sugar, flour, orange peel, and milk. Place rhubarb on the baked crust and pour the egg mixture over all. Bake 45 minutes or until rhubarb is tender.

To prepare meringue: Beat egg whites until stiff. Gradually beat in sugar and vanilla; beat until soft peaks form. Spread over rhubarb. Return to oven; bake 10 minutes or until golden brown. Makes 8 to 10 portions.

BASIC PIE PASTRY

Crust can be seasoned in many delicious ways.

1 cup shortening
1 tablespoon unsalted
  margarine or butter
3 cups all-purpose flour

1 tablespoon granulated
  sugar
¼ cup ice water

Preheat oven to 450° F. Cut shortening and margarine into flour that has been combined with sugar. Add just enough ice water to hold pastry together when stirred with a fork. Fit and trim to size in pie or tart pans. Bake about 12 minutes; reduce heat to 350° F. and continue baking until lightly browned. Makes 3 pie shells.

VARIATIONS: Season flour with grated nutmeg, orange rind, cinnamon, or pumpkin pie spices before blending in water; or substitute lemon or orange juice for water.

APPLE MACAROON PIE

Coconut tops this single-crust pie.

FILLING:

1 9-inch unbaked Basic Pie
  Pastry (see recipe, above)
4 cups pared, sliced apples
½ cup granulated sugar
1 tablespoon flour

1 teaspoon cinnamon
2 teaspoons lemon juice
2 tablespoons unsalted
  butter or margarine

TOPPING:

1⅓ cups flaked coconut
½ cup granulated sugar
1 egg, well beaten

¼ cup reconstituted low-
  sodium dry milk
½ teaspoon vanilla

To prepare filling: Preheat oven to 425° F. Arrange apples in pie shell. Combine sugar, flour, and cinnamon and pour over apples. Sprinkle with lemon juice. Dot with butter or margarine. Bake 20 minutes.

To prepare topping: Combine coconut, sugar, egg, milk, and vanilla. Spread on top of baked filling. Reduce oven to 350° F. Bake 30 more minutes, or until apples are tender. Makes 1 pie.

DOROTHY'S PEACH PIE

Quick and easy to prepare.

1 cup (or less) granulated
sugar
3 tablespoons flour
⅛ teaspoon cinnamon
⅛ teaspoon nutmeg
1 9-inch unbaked Basic Pie

Pastry (see recipe, page
122)
6 large peaches, quartered
2 tablespoons unsalted
butter or margarine

Preheat oven to 400° F. In a bowl combine sugar, flour, and
spices; sprinkle half the mixture in the bottom of the pastry
shell. Arrange peaches in a single layer over the top. Sprinkle
with remaining sugar mixture. Dot with butter or margarine
and bake 55 to 60 minutes or until juice thickens and the
crust is browned. Makes 1 pie.

NATURAL APPLE PIE

A nice, tart Granny Smith apple is good for this.

6–7 large apples, peeled and
thinly sliced
⅔ cup granulated sugar
1 teaspoon nutmeg (freshly
grated is preferable)
½ teaspoon cinnamon
Grated rind of 1 lemon
1 tablespoon fresh lemon
juice

Salt-free pastry for 9-inch
double-crust pie
Melted unsalted
margarine or low-sodium
milk
Vanilla or cinnamon
sugar

Preheat oven to 450° F. In a large bowl blend apples, sugar,
nutmeg, cinnamon, lemon rind, and juice. Fit rolled-out bottom pastry crust loosely into an 8-inch or 9-inch pie plate with
a slight overhang all around.

Pour in filling, mounding it in the center. Moisten trimmed
edge of pastry with water and place top crust over apple mix.
Seal edges. Prick top with fork points or knife slashes to allow
steam to escape. Brush with unsalted margarine or reconstituted low-sodium milk. Dust with vanilla sugar or cinnamon
sugar. Bake 10 minutes, then lower heat to 325° F. for 40 to 45
minutes. Pie is done when the filling is soft. Makes 1 pie.

SQUASH PEANUT PIE

A nutty coating glazes the top.

1 9-inch unbaked Basic Pie Pastry (see recipe, page 122)
6 tablespoons unsalted butter or margarine
½ cup plus 2 tablespoons firmly packed light brown sugar
1½ teaspoons pumpkin pie spice
2 eggs, lightly beaten

¼ cup low-sodium dairy sour cream
1 cup cooked mashed winter squash
1¾ cups reconstituted low-sodium milk
2 teaspoons pure vanilla extract
1 cup chopped unsalted peanuts

Preheat oven to 400° F. Prick bottom and sides of pie shell. Bake for 10 minutes; set aside to cool.

In a medium bowl cream 4 tablespoons of the butter or margarine with ½ cup brown sugar and pumpkin pie spice. Add eggs; mix well. Blend in sour cream. Gradually blend in squash, milk, vanilla extract. Pour into reserved pie shell. Bake for 15 minutes; remove from oven.

Meanwhile, in a small saucepan melt remaining 2 tablespoons butter. Stir in remaining 2 tablespoons brown sugar; cook and stir over low heat until sugar is dissolved. Remove from heat. Add peanuts; stir until well coated; spoon over pie filling.

Lower oven temperature to 325° F. Return pie to oven; bake until a knife inserted into the center comes out clean, about 40 minutes. Cool completely before serving. Makes 1 pie—6 to 8 portions.

BANANA CREPES

Peaches or pears could be substituted.

⅓ cup unsalted butter or margarine
½ cup orange marmalade
1 tablespoon sugar
1 tablespoon cornstarch

3 large bananas, sliced
8 warm Basic Crepes (see recipe, page 107)
Nutmeg

In a saucepan heat butter and marmalade, stirring constantly, until marmalade melts. In a bowl combine sugar and cornstarch; slowly stir into butter and marmalade. Cook over medium heat, stirring constantly, until mixture is smooth and bubbly. Remove from heat. Fold in bananas.

Spoon mixture onto center of crepes; roll. Serve with confectioners' sugar or dairy sour cream. Sprinkle with nutmeg. Makes 8 portions.

CHOCOLATE MOUSSE

Low in sodium but there are 37 milligrams per serving.

1 12-ounce package semisweet chocolate pieces
½ cup boiling water

2 teaspoons angostura bitters
4 egg yolks
4 egg whites, stiffly beaten

In a blender, combine chocolate pieces, boiling water, bitters, and egg yolks. Whirl until smooth and cool to room temperature.

Beat egg whites in a bowl until stiff. Fold in chocolate mixture. Spoon mixture into serving dishes. Chill for several hours. Makes 6 portions.

CREAM PUFFS

Great for hors d'oeuvres as well as desserts.

½ cup water
½ stick unsalted butter or margarine

½ cup all-purpose flour
2 eggs, room temperature

Preheat oven to 450° F. In a 1-quart saucepan, bring water and margarine to a boil. Remove from stove and add flour all at once. Add eggs one at a time, beating well after each addition. Continue beating until batter is glossy.

Drop scant tablespoons of batter on greased baking sheet, but do not pat puffs down. Bake 10 minutes. Reduce heat to 325° F. and bake another 30 minutes. To test cream puffs, remove one at end of baking time. If it deflates somewhat, return it to oven and bake 3 to 5 minutes longer. Makes 13 to 14 small puffs.

To serve, cut off tops, fill centers with fresh fruit or Custard Filling (see recipe below). Set tops back on and serve plain, with your favorite glaze, with frosting drizzled over them, or with chocolate sauce.

VARIATION: Make tiny ones to serve as appetizers filled with chicken or shrimp salad.

CUSTARD FILLING:

2 eggs
1 tablespoon cornstarch
2 cups reconstituted low-sodium milk

½ cup granulated sugar
1 teaspoon vanilla extract
½ teaspoon almond extract

In a 1-quart saucepan beat eggs, add cornstarch, stir in milk and sugar. Add vanilla and almond extract. Blend mixture until completely smooth. Bring to a boil over medium heat, stirring constantly with a whisk. It will thicken in about 10 minutes. Remove from heat and cool. Chill several hours before using. Makes 2 cups, enough for 13–14 small puffs.

NOTE: One egg may be used if you are cutting down on cholesterol, but *do not use egg substitutes.*

POACHED SPICED PEACHES

Serve with main course or as a dessert.

1½ cups granulated sugar	6 whole cloves
1½ cups water	6 whole allspice
1½ cups burgundy wine or black grape juice	8–10 firm ripe peaches or nectarines
2 tablespoons lemon juice	
2 sticks (4 inches each) cinnamon	

In a large saucepan combine sugar, water, wine, lemon juice, cinnamon, cloves, and allspice. Bring to the boiling point. Reduce heat and simmer, uncovered, for 15 minutes.

Drop peaches or nectarines into boiling water for 30 seconds; remove skin. Add peaches to spiced syrup in saucepan; poach until tender, about 20 minutes, turning once.

Remove peaches to a serving dish. Reduce syrup by cooking rapidly for about 3 minutes. Strain out spices from syrup except cinnamon sticks; pour syrup over peaches; chill for several hours, turning once. Makes 6 to 10 portions.

CRUNCHY CEREAL

A great combination for breakfast, as a fruit or ice cream topping, or just eating straight out of the container as a snack.

2½ cups rolled oats (regular cooking)	½ cup wheat germ
½ cup coarsely chopped unsalted nuts	¼ cup firmly packed light brown sugar
½ cup toasted sesame seeds*	¼ cup vegetable oil
½ cup reconstituted low-sodium milk	2½ teaspoons ground cinnamon
	½ teaspoon ground allspice

Preheat oven to 300° F. In a large bowl combine oats, nuts, sesame seeds, milk, and wheat germ.

In a small bowl combine brown sugar, oil, cinnamon, and allspice; mix with dry ingredients; spread in a jelly-roll pan. Bake, stirring occasionally, until toasted, about 1 hour. Makes about 4 cups.

*To toast sesame seeds, place in a skillet over moderate heat until golden, stirring often.

APPENDIX

SODIUM CONTENT OF VARIOUS LOW-SODIUM FOODS

Uncooked weight	Milligrams sodium	Uncooked weight	Milligrams sodium
MEAT AND POULTRY			
4 ounces beef	80.0	4 ounces pork	64.0
4 ounces chicken (dark)	124.0	4 ounces rabbit	53.0
4 ounces chicken (white)	89.0	4 ounces sweetbreads	100.0
4 ounces duck (breast)	80.0	4 ounces tongue	90.0
4 ounces duck (leg)	108.0	4 ounces turkey (dark)	104.0
4 ounces lamb	100.0	4 ounces turkey (white)	48.0
4 ounces liver (calf)	125.0	4 ounces veal	110.0
FRESH FISH			
3 ounces bass	75.0	3 ounces mackerel	60.0
3 ounces bluefish	75.0	3 medium oysters	90.0
3 ounces cod	88.0	3 ounces salmon	90.0
3 ounces flounder	64.0	3 ounces sole	100.0
3 ounces haddock	68.0	3 ounces swordfish	90.0
3 ounces halibut	60.0	3 ounces trout	60.0
		3 ounces tuna	90.0
FRESH VEGETABLES			
6 stalks asparagus	2.0	10 pods okra	1.0
½ cup green and wax beans	1.0	1 medium onion	6.0
		1 tablespoon parsley	1.0
½ cup lima beans	1.0	½ cup peas	0.7
½ cup broccoli	10.1	½ green pepper	0.5
5 Brussels sprouts	5.6	1 white potato	4.0
½ cup shredded cabbage	6.4	1 sweet potato	12.0
		1 cup pumpkin	2.0
½ cup carrot slices	24.0	3 radishes	6.0
½ cup cauliflower	18.0	½ cup summer squash	0.6
1 ear sweet corn	3.0	½ cup winter squash	0.6
½ cucumber	3.6	½ tomato	1.5
½ eggplant	8.4	½ cup cooked turnip greens	10.0
4 escarole leaves	3.6		
¼ head Iceberg lettuce	12.0	½ cup cooked yellow turnips	5.0
8 large mushrooms	10.0		
		½ cup watercress	11.0

Uncooked weight	Milligrams sodium	Uncooked weight	Milligrams sodium
FRESH FRUIT			
1 apple (skinned)	2.0	¼ cup lemon juice	
1 apricot	0.4	and pulp	1.0
½ avocado	3.0	1 mango	4.0
1 banana	1.4	1 orange	2.0
½ cup blackberries	2.0	1 papaya	6.0
½ cup blueberries	1.0	1 peach	2.0
¼ cantaloupe	6.0	1 pear	2.0
½ cup cherries	3.0	½ cup pineapple	1.0
½ cup grated coconut	9.2	1 plum	0.6
1 cup cranberries	1.0	1 cup raspberries	1.0
½ cup currants	1.3	1 cup rhubarb	2.0
½ grapefruit	3.0	10 strawberries	0.8
10 grapes	1.2	1 tangerine	0.6
		8 ounces watermelon	0.6
DAIRY PRODUCTS			
1 tablespoon sweet (un-		1 cup plain yogurt	117.0
salted) butter	0.7	1 cup fruit yogurt	88.0
1 cup nonfat unsalted		1 ounce low-sodium	
buttermilk	120.0	cheese	2.7
1 cup reconstituted evap-		¼ cup low-sodium cot-	
orated milk	126.0	tage cheese	12.0
1 cup skim milk	127.9	1 tablespoon cream	5.7
1 cup whole milk	122.0	1 tablespoon sour cream	5.7
1 cup reconstituted low-		1 tablespoon milk	7.6
sodium dry milk	7.0	1 egg	68.0
1 cup low-sodium fresh		1 egg yolk	13.0
milk	12.0	1 egg white	55.0
BREAD			
1 slice low-sodium bread	4.0	1 low-sodium roll	4.0
1 low-sodium melba toast	1.6	1 matzoh	0.2
CEREALS AND PASTA			
½ cup uncooked barley	3.0	½ cup cooked Ralston	0.4
1 cup low-sodium		½ cup cooked rolled oats	0.4
cornflakes	2.0	1 cup puffed rice	0.5
½ cup cooked cornmeal	0.5	½ cup uncooked white	
1 cup popcorn	0.8	rice	2.0
½ cup cooked Cream of		½ cup cooked spaghetti	1.5
Wheat	1.0	1 tablespoon tapioca	1.0
½ cup cooked farina	4.0	1 cup puffed wheat	1.0
½ cup cooked macaroni	1.0	½ cup cooked Wheatena	0.4
½ cup cooked Maltex	2.0	1 tablespoon wheat germ	0.1
		1 shredded wheat biscuit	4.0

Uncooked weight	Milligrams sodium	Uncooked weight	Milligrams sodium

MISCELLANEOUS FOOD

1 tablespoon cornstarch	0.5	1 tablespoon unflavored gelatin	3.6
1 cup flour	2.7	1 tablespoon cider or distilled vinegar	negligible
1 tablespoon flour	0.1		
1 teaspoon cream of tartar	8.0	1 tablespoon red wine vinegar	4.0
1 tablespoon compressed yeast	0.6	1 tablespoon white wine vinegar	5.0

FATS AND OILS

1 tablespoon low-sodium margarine	1.5	¼ cup olive oil	0.15
		1 tablespoon olive oil	negligible
1 tablespoon low-sodium mayonnaise	6.0	¼ cup safflower oil	0.15
		¼ cup soybean oil	0.15
¼ cup corn oil	0.15	¼ cup vegetable shortening	0.4

SWEETS

1 square unsweetened chocolate	3.0	1 marshmallow	3.1
		1 tablespoon brown sugar	3.4
1 tablespoon honey	1.5	1 tablespoon powdered sugar	0.1
1 tablespoon jam or jelly without added preservatives	1.0	1 cup white sugar	0.8
1 tablespoon pure maple syrup	2.8	1 tablespoon white sugar	negligible

BEVERAGES

1 teaspoon cocoa	2.0	1 teaspoon instant Postum	0.4
1 teaspoon instant coffee	1.7	1 teaspoon Sanka	0.1
1 tablespoon regular coffee	1.5	1 teaspoon tea	0.1

FRUIT JUICES

1 cup apple cider	2.0	1 cup orange juice	5.0
1 cup apple juice	12.0	1 cup pineapple juice	1.2
1 cup apricot juice	8.0	1 cup prune juice	4.0
1 cup cranberry juice	6.0	1 cup tangerine juice	4.0
1 cup grape juice	8.0	1 cup fresh tomato juice	12.0
1 cup grapefruit juice	4.0	1 cup canned low-sodium tomato juice	12.0
1 cup lemon juice	4.0		

CARBONATED BEVERAGES

6½ ounces Coca-Cola	1.8	8 ounces ginger ale	18.4
7 ounces 7-Up	13.9	8 ounces club soda	1.7

Uncooked weight	Milligrams sodium	Uncooked weight	Milligrams sodium

MILKS

Uncooked weight	Milligrams sodium	Uncooked weight	Milligrams sodium
1 cup whole milk	122.0	1 cup low-sodium dry milk, liquified	7.0
1 cup skim milk	127.9	1 cup low-sodium fresh milk	12.0

ALCOHOLIC BEVERAGES

Uncooked weight	Milligrams sodium	Uncooked weight	Milligrams sodium
1 cup beer	2.6–11.4	1 cup dry sauterne	22.0
1 ounce brandy	1.3	3 ounces sake	4.0
3 ounces champagne	3.0	1 ounce sherry	4.6
3 ounces Dubonnet	4.0	1 ounce dry or sweet vermouth	1.0
1 ounce gin	0.2	1 ounce whiskey, bourbon, rye, tequila, vodka	0.9
3 ounces sweet or dry marsala	4.0	1 cup red table wine	16.0
3 ounces port	3.0		
1 ounce rum	0.5		

NUTS

Uncooked weight	Milligrams sodium	Uncooked weight	Milligrams sodium
4 almonds	1.0	10 hazelnuts	0.5
4 Brazil nuts	4.0	10 peanuts	1.6
4 cashews	2.0	4 whole pecans	1.6
4 chestnuts	0.67	4 walnuts	1.3

DRIED VEGETABLES

Uncooked weight	Milligrams sodium	Uncooked weight	Milligrams sodium
½ cup split peas	25.0	½ cup navy beans	1.0
½ cup lentils	4.0	½ cup kidney beans	2.8
½ cup soybeans	4.0	½ cup pea beans	1.0

CANNED FRUITS

Uncooked weight	Milligrams sodium	Uncooked weight	Milligrams sodium
½ cup applesauce	3.6	½ cup grapefruit	3.0
½ cup apricots	5.0	2 peach halves	3.0
½ cup cherries	1.0	2 pear halves	2.0
½ cup cranberry sauce	1.2	2 small pineapple slices	1.0
		3 plums	3.0

DRIED FRUITS

Uncooked weight	Milligrams sodium	Uncooked weight	Milligrams sodium
2 apricots	2.5	4 prunes	3.0
5 dates	negligible	1 tablespoon raisins	3.0
1 peach	5.0	2 large figs	16.0

COMPANIES THAT SUPPLY SPECIAL DIETARY PRODUCTS

Abbott Laboratories
Pharmaceutical Products
  Division
Abbott Park
North Chicago, IL 60064

Adelph's Ltd.
1800 West Magnolia Boulevard
Burbank, CA 91503

Anderson Clayton Foods
W.L. Clayton Research Center
3333 North Central Expressway
Richardson, TX 75080

Bernard Food Industries, Inc.
1125 Hartrey Avenue
P.O. Box 1497
Evanston, IL 60204
  Low-sodium foods, mixes,
sauces, pie fillings, etc.

California Canners & Growers
3100 Ferry Building
San Francisco, CA 94106
  Some sugar-free and some
salt-free canned foods

Campbell Soup Company
Campbell Place
Camden, NJ 08101

Chicago Dietetic Supply, Inc.
P.O. Box 529
La Grange, IL 60525
  Foods for low-sodium/salt-free
diets

Clayco Foods, Inc.
1775 Broadway
New York, NY 10019
  Foods for low-sodium/salt-free
diets

Diamond Crystal Salt Company
10 Burlington Avenue
Wilmington, MA 01887
  Salt substitute and sugar
substitute

D. M. Doyle Pharmaceutical
  Company
5320 West 23rd Street
Minneapolis, MN 55416

General Foods
250 North Street
White Plains, NY 10602

Geoghegan's Dietetic Foods
Wholesale Grocers & Importers,
  Inc.
8835 South Greenwood Avenue
Chicago, IL 60619
  Dietetic, low-calorie, and
special diet foods

Hain Pure Food Company, Inc.
P.O. Box 54841 Terminal Annex
Los Angeles, CA 90054
  Mayonnaise, dressings, etc.
made salt-free

Kingsmith Foods Ltd.
280 Nantucket Boulevard
Scarborough 705 Ontario,
  Canada

Low-Sodium Dairy Products
346 Rose Avenue
Venice, CA 90291

MCP Foods, Inc.
424 South Atchison Street
Anaheim, CA 92805
  A jelling mix for sugar
restricted diets

Morton Salt Division
Morton Norwick
110 N. Wacker Drive
Chicago, IL 60654

Quaker Oats Company
Home Economics Department
Merchandise Mart Plaza
Chicago, IL 60654

Tillie Lewis Foods, Inc.
Drawer J
Stockton, CA 95201

Van Brode Milling Company,
  Inc.
Cameron Street
Clinton, MA 01510

BIBLIOGRAPHY

American Heart Association. "Your 500 Milligrams Sodium Diet"; "Your 1000 Milligrams Sodium Diet"; "Your Mild Sodium-Restricted Diet."

American Spice Trade Association. "A History of Spices"; "How to Use Spices"; "Spices."

Bagg, Elma W. *Cooking Without a Grain of Salt.* Garden City, New York: Doubleday, 1980.

Bradley, Alice V., M.S. *Tables of Food Value.* Peoria, Illinois: Chas. A. Bennett, 1931.

Brunswick, J. Peter; Love, Dorothy; and Weinberg, Assa, M.D. *How to Live 365 Days a Year the Salt-Free Way.* New York: Bantam Books, 1980.

Kempner, Walter, M.D. *Radical Dietary Treatment of Hypertensive and Arteriosclerotic Vascular Disease, Heart and Kidney Disease, and Vascular Retinopathy.* Durham, North Carolina: Duke University School of Medicine.

Laragh, John H., M.D., professor of medicine, director of Cardiovascular Center and Hypertension Center; chief, Cardiology Division, Department of Medicine, New York Hospital-Cornell Medical Center: Testimony presented April 13, 1981 to the Committee of Science and Technology, U.S. House of Representatives, Washington, D.C.

Lipman, Arthur G., PharmD, "Sodium Content of Some Commonly Used Antacids," *Modern Medicine,* January 30–February 15, 1980.

Macklin, Roberta. *Substitute, It's Fun.* San Antonio: The Naylor Company.

Margie, Joyce Daly, M.S.; Anderson, Carl F., M.D.; Nelson, Ralph A., M.D., Ph.D.; Hunt, James C., M.D. *The Mayo Clinic Renal Diet Cookbook.* New York: Golden Press.

Margie, Joyce Daly, M.S.; Hunt, James C., M.D. *Living with High Blood Pressure: The Hypertension Diet Cookbook.* Radnor, Pennsylvania: Chilton, 1979.

Marsh, Ann C., Klippstein, Ruth V., and Kaplan, Syvil D. "The Sodium Content of Your Food," *Home and Garden Bulletin no. 233.* Washington, D.C.: United States Department of Agriculture, 1980.

McCane, R. A. and Widdowson, E. M. *The Chemical Composition of Foods.* Brooklyn, New York: Chemical Publishing, 1947.

The McCormick Spices of the World Cookbook. New York: McGraw-Hill, 1964.

National Research Council, "Sodium-Restricted Diets." National Academy of Science Publication no. 32, July 1954.

Peterson, Skinner, Strong, *Elements of Food Biochemistry.* New York: Prentice-Hall, 1943.

Sherman, Henry C., Ph.D., Sc.D. *Chemistry of Food and Nutrition.* New York: Macmillan, 1946.

Small, Marvin. *The Special Diet Cook Book.* New York: Hawthorn Books, 1969.

Sodium and Potassium Analyses of Foods and Waters. Evansville, Indiana: Mead Johnson Research Laboratory, 1947.

Taylor, Clara Mae, Ph.D. *Food Value in Shares and Weights.* 2nd ed., New York: Macmillan, 1959.

Thorburn, Anna Houston and Turner, Phyllis. *Living Salt Free and Easy.* New York: New American Library, 1975.

Watt, Bernice K. and Merrill, Annabel L. *Composition of Foods.* Washington, D.C.: United States Department of Agriculture, 1975.

The Yearbook of Agriculture 1959. Washington, D.C.: United States Department of Agriculture, 1959.

INDEX

breads (*cont.*)
 Spiced Cranberry-Nut Bread, 118
 See also baked goods
Brookhaven National Laboratories,
  14, 15
butter, 50-51
 how to make, salt-free, 51
 sodium content of, 130
butter churns, 51
buttermilk
 how to make, salt-free, 51
 sodium content of, 130

cakes
 Fresh Tomato Cake, 119
 Spiced Chocolate Zucchini Cake,
  120
canned foods. *See* packaged and
  canned foods
canning, without salt, 46
caraway seeds, 58
carbonated beverages, 36, 45
 sodium content of, 131
cardamom, 58-59
cardiovascular disease, 23. *See also*
  hypertension
Carrot-Stuffed Meat Loaf, 88
Carrots with Orange Sauce, 110
Cauliflower Salad, Raw, 85
celery seeds, 59
Cereal, Crunchy, 127
cereals, 37
 sodium content of, 130
charley horses, 23
cheddar and potato chowder, 81
cheese dishes
 Cheese-Stuffed Green Peppers,
  104
 Potato Cheddar Chowder, 81
 See also cottage cheese; dairy
  products
chicken and chicken dishes, 99-103
 Chicken Mediterranean, 99
 Curried Chicken, 100
 as "eat-your-fill" food, 39
 Lemon Chicken, 101
 Marinated Chicken Salad, 101
 in restaurants, 41
 sodium content of, 129
 Stir-Fried Chicken and Vegetables, 102
 Swank Chicken Chili, 102
 Tandoori Chicken, 103

Chicken Mediterranean, 99
Chili, Swank Chicken, 102
chili powder, 60
Chinese dishes
 in restaurants, 41
 Stir-Fried Chicken and Vegetables, 102
 Vegetables, Oriental, 113
chlorine, 23
chocolate, 46
 how to make, salt-free, 51
 sodium content of, 131
Chocolate Mousse, 125
Chocolate Zucchini Cake, Spiced,
  120
cholesterol, 20, 23
Chowder, Potato Cheddar, 81
cigarette smoking, 21
cinnamon, 60-61
citrus and onion salad, 83
citrus peel, 65-66
Claiborne, Craig, 45
Clam and Walnut Stuffed Mushrooms, 110
clams, 29
cloves, 61
cocoa, 46, 51
 sodium content of, 131
Cod with a Tang, 96
coffee, sodium content of, 131
companies supplying dietary products, 133-34
Consumer Reports, 33
cookies
 Lace Doughnuts, 120
coriander, 62
cottage cheese
 commercial, 51
 how to make, salt-free, 52
cramps, painful, 26
Cranberry-Nut Bread, Spiced, 118
cream, 29, 47, 52
 sodium content of, 130
Creamed Eggs and Mushrooms, 104
Cream Puffs, 126
Crepes, Banana, 125
Crepes, Basic, 107
Crepes, Vegetable, 108
Crunchy Cereal, 127
cucumber raita, 84
Cucumber Rings, Sautéed, 112
Cucumbers, Frozen, 111
cumin seeds, 62-63

water, bottled, 45-46
water supply, sodium in, 34-35
wines, 38
   as flavoring ingredients, 79
   sodium content of, 132
Worcestershire sauce, 79

yogurt
   in cucumber raita, 84

how to make, salt-free, 54
   sodium content of, 130
yogurt makers, 54

Zucchini, Apricot Stuffed, 109
Zucchini Cake, Spiced Chocolate, 120
Zucchini Soup, 82